This book belongs to:

_____

LEISURE ARTS, INC.
Little Rock, Arkansas

Sweeter than the Rose

EDITORIAL STAFF

Editor-in Chief: Anne Van Wagner Childs. *Executive Director:* Sandra Graham Case. *Executive Editor:* Susan Frantz Wiles. *Publications Director:* Carla Bentley. *Creative Art Director:* Gloria Bearden. *Production Art Director:* Melinda Stout. PRODUCTION — *Managing Editor:* Susan White Sullivan. *Senior Editor:* Carla A. Jones. *Project Coordinators:* Gail Sharp and Andrea Ahlen. DESIGN — *Design Director:* Patricia Wallenfang Sowers. *Designers:* Donna Waldrip Pittard and Diana Heien Suttle. EDITORIAL — *Associate Editor:* Linda L. Trimble. *Senior Editor:* Laurie S. Rodwell. *Editorial Writer:* Tammi Williamson-Bradley. *Copy Editor:* Laura Lee Stewart. ART — *Book/Magazine Art Director:* Diane M. Ghegan. *Senior Production Artist:* Stephen L. Mooningham. *Production Artist:* Mark A. Hawkins. *Art Assistants:* Laura K. Bushmiaer, Deborah Taylor Choate, Susan Dailey, Hubrith Esters, Leslie Loring Krebs, Valerie K. Martin, Noelle Tinnin, Guniz Ustun, and Andy Warren. *Creative Art Assistant:* Judith Howington Merritt. *Photography Stylists:* Christina Tiano and Karen Smart Hall. *Typesetters:* Cindy Lumpkin and Stephanie Cordero. ADVERTISING AND DIRECT MAIL — *Copywriters:* Steven M. Cooper, Marla Shivers, and Tena Kelley Vaughn. *Designer:* Rhonda H. Hestir. *Art Director:* Jeff Curtis. *Artist:* Linda Lovette Smart.

BUSINESS STAFF

Publisher: Steve Patterson. *Controller:* Tom Siebenmorgen. *Retail Sales Director:* Richard Tignor. *Retail Marketing Director:* Pam Stebbins. *Retail Customer Services Director:* Margaret Sweetin. *Marketing Manager:* Russ Barnett. *Executive Director of Marketing and Circulation:* Guy A. Crossley. *Fulfillment Manager:* Byron L. Taylor. *Print Production:* Nancy Reddick Lister and Laura Lockhart.

CREDITS

PHOTOGRAPHY: Ken West, Larry Pennington, and Mark Mathews of Peerless Photography, Little Rock, Arkansas; and Jerry R. Davis of Jerry Davis Photography, Little Rock, Arkansas. COLOR SEPARATIONS: Magna IV Color Imaging of Little Rock, Arkansas. CUSTOM FRAMING: Nelda and Carlton Newby of Creative Framers, North Little Rock, Arkansas. PHOTO LOCATIONS: The homes of Carol Clawson, Shirley Held, Trisha Hendrix, Nancy Gunn Porter, and Philip Quick.

Library of Congress Catalog Number 93-85969
International Standard Book Number 0-942237-34-X

INTRODUCTION

The natural beauty of flowers, with their delicate petals and sweet fragrances, captivated the souls of the sentimental Victorians. Many a hopeful suitor wooed and won the heart of his beloved with artfully arranged bouquets of freshly cut blossoms. Genteel ladies of the era lovingly cultivated lush flower gardens, often reproducing the beautiful blooms with needle and thread. Sweeter Than the Rose offers a lovely collection of feminine floral projects that bring the charm of this gentler time to our lives. Inspired by antique artwork, the designs celebrate the innocent sweetness of children paired with the timeless appeal of flowers. These magical scenes from the past add a bit of enchantment to our homes, taking us to a place where cherubic children frolic with fanciful fairies and brilliant butterflies, and velvety roses, shy violets, and pretty pansies bloom year 'round. As you turn the pages of this very special volume, you'll discover all the delights of a Victorian flower garden.

TABLE OF CONTENTS

5

Teatime Roses

An afternoon tea party in the rose garden brings to mind genteel images from years gone by. Providing a welcome respite from the busy day, the soothing ritual of pouring tea into dainty cups calms the soul and refreshes the spirit. Fragile roses and violets, captured with needle and thread, lend feminine charm to teatime accessories in this lovely collection. Surrounded by the soft beauty of flowers, we can enjoy a quiet hour of gentle delights.

Charts on pages 50-51

7

Charts on page 50

There are few hours in life more agreeable than the hour dedicated to the ceremony known as afternoon tea.

— HENRY JAMES

Chart on page 51

Flights of fancy

Transporting us back to a place where rosy-cheeked
fairies rode in leafy chariots drawn by butterfly steeds,
memories of childhood bring to mind beloved tales of Faerie.
During those carefree years, when possibilities were as endless
as the imagination, flights of fantasy took us often to those
magical lands that were invisible to grown-up eyes. In
this collection, frolicking fairies and brilliant butterflies are
nostalgic reminders of the innocent joys of youth.

Chart on page 56

Charts on page 54

Chart on page 53

When the first baby laughed for the first time, the laugh broke into a thousand pieces and they all went skipping about, and that was the beginning of fairies.

— *SIR JAMES MATTHEW BARRIE*

Chart on page 56

Chart on page 55

14

*Fluttering from flower to flower, bright-winged butterflies
bring a feeling of lightheartedness to the garden. A colorful
bouquet blooms on a sweater, and pretty throw pillows
bring a breath of springtime indoors.*

Charts on pages 53 and 55

Violets so fair

These little flowers, that in the shadow grow,
Half hidden by the green leaves round them springing,
Although they hold their pretty heads so low,
Are just the flowers my message to be bringing.

Sweet violets, whose fragrance is the first
In garden and in woodland wild awaking,
Before the birds their new songs have rehearsed,
Before the green trees into leaf are breaking —

They speak my wish for you — a fragrant year,
By hope and happy promise sweetly scented;
And ever, ever when the skies are drear,
The perfume of a heart with life contented.

No soft prayer, no stately measured phrase,
Sonorous words of grandeur here shall meet you:
A simple wish that grew in happy ways
Is all I send — Sweet violets to greet you.

— CLIFTON LINGHAM

Chart on pages 58-59

Chart on page 61

Charts on pages 60 and 62

Shy violets blossom in this sweet collection. Twining 'round a fabric mat, they create a lovely setting for an heirloom photograph. Dainty accessories such as scented sachets, a lacy handkerchief, and embroidered bookmarks bring beauty to your private haven.

Charts on page 63

19

Discovering a tiny violet peeping from beneath a leaf is always a delight. Inspiring us to seek out such unexpected pleasures, a sentimental verse is surrounded by flowers and decorative stitches. A violet-trimmed blouse or sweater adds gentle romance to your wardrobe.

Charts on page 62

Hath the pearl less whiteness
Because of its birth?
Hath the violet
less brightness
For growing
near earth?

—Moore

Chart on page 60

Chart on page 63

21

Blushing Rose

Blushed with color, velvety red roses have long
been acclaimed as the queen of the flower garden.
The richly hued blossoms are also a favorite among
suitors, bringing an added breath of romance to
courtship bouquets. This rosy collection pays
tribute to these lovely messengers of love.

Each fairy breath of Summer, as it blows,
With loveliness inspires the blushing rose.

Chart on pages 64-65

Charts on pages 66-67

Charts on pages 64 and 66-67

Emblems of love and beauty, roses are cherished as tokens of affection. A basket of luxurious blossoms adds richness to our ruffled pillow, and an old-fashioned hanging pocket can be filled with blooms and displayed on a wall or hung over a drawer knob. The sentimental flowers also adorn simple Shaker boxes and a pretty porcelain jar — lovely for holding potpourri or petals from a keepsake bouquet.

Charts on pages 66-67

Chart on pages 70-71

Gather ye Rosebuds

With their dewy skin and rosy cheeks, children
are much like flowers. The Victorians adored these little cherubs,
often pairing them with luxurious blossoms in beautifully detailed
illustrations. Created as a tribute to the innocence of youth, this
collection of roses is perfect for a lady's hideaway.

Chart on page 74

*W*omen of yesteryear loved
to gather fresh flowers to
adorn their homes, savoring the
sweet fragrances that wafted
through every room. Roses
were especially prized for their
rich color and heady scent.
Here, a scattering of blooms
brings a breath of spring
to a ruffled afghan and a
dainty keepsake box.

Of all flowers
Methinks a Rose is best ...
It is the very emblem of a maid;
For when the west wind
courts her gently,
How modestly she blows
and paints the sun
With her chaste blushes.

— BEAUMONT AND FLETCHER

Charts on page 74

*Spilling out of a basket or gathered
in a trailing bouquet, roses are the crowning
glory of the garden. Such lovely blossoms
bring romance to a simple sweater and add
elegance to a hand mirror. Captured
on linen, a mixture of full-blown blooms
and delicate buds provides a lasting
reminder of the beauty of nature.*

Chart on page 74

Chart on page 69

Chart on page 73

Gather
ye rosebuds
while ye may,
Old time
is still a-flying;
And this same flower
that smiles today,
Tomorrow
will be dying.
HERRICK

Chart on page 72

Charts on page 75

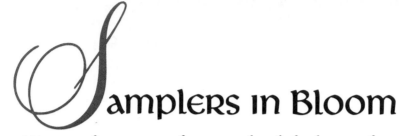

Samplers in Bloom

*Women of yesteryear often reproduced the beauty they
saw in bloom around them in their embroidery, capturing the
delicate blossoms with needle and thread. With their timeless
promise of renewal, spring flowers add a gentle touch to our
samplers, complementing the traditional letters and verses.
Embellished with a potpourri of floral designs, this sentimental
collection features a variety of old-fashioned decorative stitches
that link us ever closer to these women of the past.*

A B C D E F G H
I J K L M N O P
Q R S T U V W X
&c. X Y Z 1924
a b c d e f g h i j k l m n
o p q r s t u v w x y z

"Where fall the
tears of love the
rose appears." Bryant

Chart on pages 76-77

Charts on pages 78 and 80

39

Delicate blossoms and feminine borders add a romantic air to accessories for the bed and bath. Borrowed from the samplers shown on the preceding pages, the dainty designs here are year-round reminders of spring's fragrant beauty.

Charts on pages 78-80

Charts on pages 78-79

Pretty sachets fill the air with the essence of flowers. A beaded cloth lines a basket of sweetly scented toiletries.

Charts on pages 78-79

Pansy Potpourri

In the language of flowers, every blossom has a special significance. Transforming even the simplest bouquets into beautiful declarations of love, these unspoken messages captured the fancy of the Victorians. Colorful pansies, symbolizing love and kind thoughts, would have been a favored choice for such sentimental offerings.

Chart on page 87

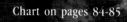

Chart on pages 84-85

Charts on pages 86-87

Also known by such picturesque names as hearts-ease and love-in-idleness, pansies bring a rainbow of color to the bedroom. A ruffled pillow and pillowcases embroidered with a pretty potpourri of pansies inspire gentle reveries and dreams of love. Keeping time with Nature, softly colored blooms twine around the face of a wooden clock.

Chart on page 86

Nostalgic notions

Genteel ladies of the Victorian Era took great pride
in their sewing and embroidery, knowing that the fine
handwork and neat, tiny stitches were reflections of their
domestic accomplishments. As needlewomen today, we share
this attention to detail and quality with our sisters of the
past. Lending a touch of enchantment to the sewing
room, this collection of accessories is adorned
with fanciful fairies and flowers.

Chart on page 92

Chart on pages 88-89

Accessories bedecked with ribbons, roses, and cherubic fairies add to the pleasures of needlework. A dainty hanging pincushion is trimmed with lace and pearls. Keeping sewing necessities close at hand, the pretty chatelaine features a playful fairy on the needle case and a decorative "S" on the scissors case. A tiny fairy diligently mends a leaf on the cover of a lovely needlework organizer.

Chart on page 90

Charts on page 92

46

Chart on page 90

47

Chart on page 92

Handmade accents spread the joys of needlework to every room. Their wings shimmering with iridescent thread, three little fairies gather 'round a morning glory gramophone to hear a sweet melody. A small embroidery hoop is the perfect spot for a sweet-faced cherub.

Chart on pages 88-89

*$\mathscr{A}$dorned with flowers, old-fashioned sewing notions,
and a delicately stitched rose, a wreath of greenery becomes
a beautiful tribute to seamstresses everywhere.*

Chart on page 92

teatime Roses

Each design was stitched on White Lugana (25 ct) over 2 fabric threads using 3 strands of floss for Cross Stitch and 1 strand for Backstitch. Instructions for all projects on page 52.

Designed by Diane Brakefield.

#3 (32w x 33h)

#2 (51w x 51h)

#1 (84w x 82h)

X	DMC	B'ST
	blanc	
	208	
	209	
	211	
	434	
2	500	
	501	
S	502	
V	503	
-	504	
	725	
	727	
X	776	
	793	
	794	
	818	
	902	/
	3350	
	3364	
	3731	
	3733	
	3747	
	3753	
	3755	
	3799	/

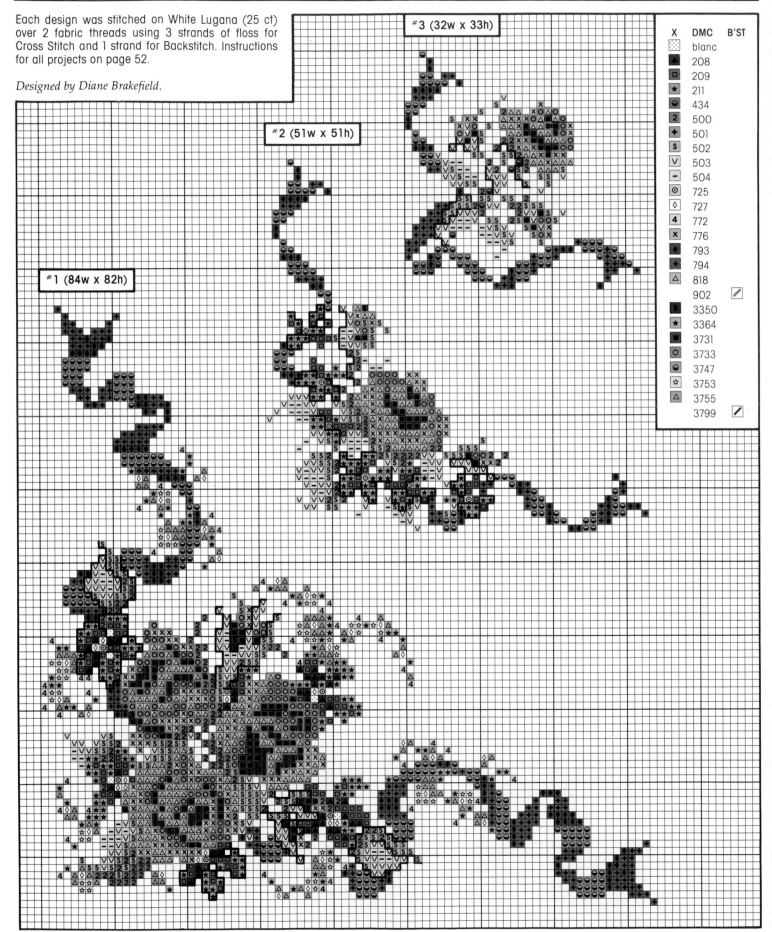

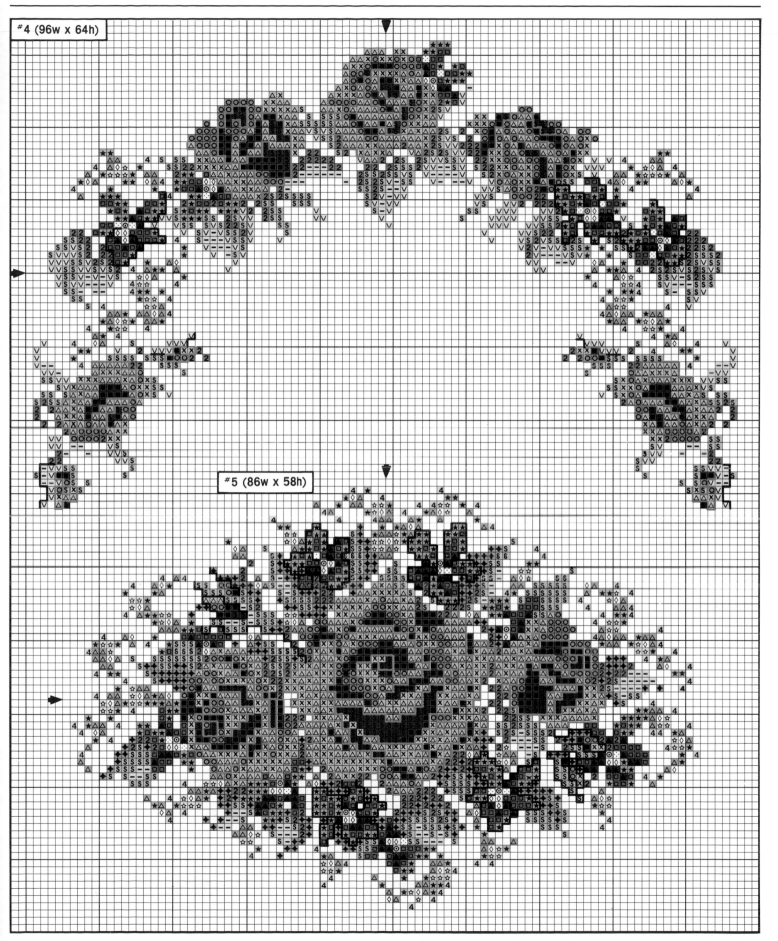

#4 (96w x 64h)

#5 (86w x 58h)

Teatime Roses

All projects were stitched over 2 fabric threads on White Lugana (25 ct) using 3 strands of floss for Cross Stitch, 1 strand of floss for Backstitch, and 1 strand of blanc DMC Pearl Cotton #12 for Nun Stitch. Refer to General Instructions, page 95, for Nun Stitch instructions.

Roses and Violets Crumb Catcher (shown on page 8, chart on page 50): Design #1 was stitched in one corner of a 27" square of fabric, 4¼" from edges of fabric.

For crumb catcher, work Nun Stitch 1⅞" from edge of fabric on all sides. Trim fabric ½" from Nun Stitch; fringe to Nun Stitch.

Roses and Violets Basket Cloth (shown on page 8, chart on page 50): Design #2 was stitched in one corner of a 20" square of fabric, 3⅛" from edges of fabric.

For basket cloth, work Nun Stitch 1½" from edge of fabric on all sides. Trim fabric ½" from Nun Stitch; fringe to Nun Stitch.

Rose Napkin (shown on page 6, chart on page 50): Design #3 was stitched in one corner of a 16" square of fabric, 3¼" from edges of fabric.

For napkin, work Nun Stitch 1½" from edge of fabric on all sides. Trim fabric ½" from Nun Stitch; fringe to Nun Stitch.

Roses and Violets Tea Cozy (shown on page 7, chart on page 51): Design #4 was stitched on a 19" x 15" piece of fabric.

For cozy, you will need tracing paper, 19" x 15" piece of coordinating fabric for backing, two 19" x 15" pieces of craft fleece, two 19" x 15" pieces of fabric for lining, 2" x 28" bias strip of fabric for cording, 28" length of ¼" dia. purchased cord, thread to match fabric, and fabric marking pencil.

For cozy pattern, fold tracing paper in half and place fold on dashed line of cozy pattern (page 96); add ½" seam allowance on all sides and trace pattern onto tracing paper. Cut out pattern; unfold and press flat. Referring to photo for placement, position pattern on wrong side of stitched piece and pin pattern in place. Use fabric marking pencil to draw around pattern; remove pattern and cut out on drawn line. Use pattern and cut **one** from backing fabric and **two each** from lining fabric and fleece.

For cozy front, match right sides and raw edges of one lining fabric piece and stitched piece; place one fleece piece on lining piece and pin in place. Using a ½" seam allowance, stitch through all layers along bottom edge; remove pins. Trim seam allowance to ¼"; turn right side out and press. Baste through all layers close to raw edges. For cozy back, repeat with backing fabric and remaining lining piece and fleece piece.

For cording, center cord on wrong side of bias strip; matching long edges, fold strip over cord. Use a zipper foot to baste along length of strip close to cord; trim seam allowance to ½". Matching raw edges, baste cording to right side of top edge on cozy front with cording extended 1" beyond bottom edges.

Matching right sides of cozy front and cozy back and beginning and ending at bottom edge, use a ½" seam allowance to sew front and back together; clip curves as needed and turn cozy right side out. On each end of cording remove 1" of basting, trim cord even with bottom edge of cozy. Turn loose ends of bias strip to inside of cozy and blind stitch in place.

Roses and Violets Tray (shown on page 9, chart on page 51): Design #5 was stitched on a 13" x 10" piece of fabric. It was inserted in a 12" x 9" purchased tray (10" x 7" oval opening).

Designed by Diane Brakefield.

Flights of Fancy

"Love Knows" Pillow (shown on page 15): The design was stitched over 2 fabric threads on a 12" x 10" piece of Ivory Lugana (25 ct) using 3 strands of floss for Cross Stitch and 1 strand for Backstitch.

For pillow, center design and trim stitched piece to measure 7½" x 6". You will also need two 13" x 11" pieces of fabric for pillow front and backing, 6" x 4½" piece of craft fleece for padding stitched piece, 2" x 29" bias strip of coordinating fabric for ¼" cord, 29" length of ¼" dia. purchased cord, 2½" x 50" (pieced as necessary) bias strip of fabric for ⅜" cord, 50" length of ⅜" dia. purchased cord, and polyester fiberfill.

Center ¼" dia. cord on wrong side of bias strip; matching long edges, fold strip over cord. Use a zipper foot to baste along length of strip close to cord; trim seam allowance to ½". Beginning at center bottom and matching raw edges, pin cording to right side of stitched piece making a ⅜" clip in seam allowance of cording at corners. Ends of cording should overlap approximately 2"; pin overlapping end out of the way. Starting 2" from beginning end of cording and ending 4" from overlapping end, baste cording to stitched piece. On overlapping end of cording, remove 2½" of basting; fold end of fabric back and trim cord so that it meets beginning end of cord. Fold end of fabric under ½"; wrap fabric over beginning end of cording.

Finish basting cording to stitched piece; press seam allowances toward stitched piece.

For pillow front, place fleece on wrong side of stitched piece (with fleece between stitched piece and seam allowance), center wrong side of stitched piece and fleece to right side of one 13" x 11" of fabric; baste in place. Using zipper foot and same color thread as cording, attach stitched piece to pillow front by sewing through all layers as close as possible to cording, taking care not to catch fabric of stitched piece.

Center ⅜" dia. cord on wrong side of bias strip; matching long edges, fold strip over cord. Baste along length of strip close to cord; trim seam allowance to ½". Matching raw edges, pin cording to right side of pillow front making a ⅜" clip in seam allowance of cording at corners. Ends of cording should overlap approximately 2"; pin overlapping end out of the way. Starting 2" from beginning end of cording and ending 4" from overlapping end, baste cording to pillow front. On overlapping end of cording, remove 2½" of basting; fold end of fabric back and trim cord so that it meets beginning end of cord. Fold end of fabric under ½"; wrap fabric over beginning end of cording. Finish basting cording to pillow front.

Matching right sides and leaving an opening for turning, use a ½" seam allowance to sew pillow front and backing fabric together. Trim seam allowances diagonally at corners; turn pillow right side out carefully pushing corners outward. Stuff pillow with polyester fiberfill and blind stitch opening closed.

Butterfly and Daisy Porcelain Jar (shown on page 13): The design was stitched over 2 fabric threads on an 8" square of Cream Belfast Linen (32 ct) using 2 strands of floss for Cross Stitch and 1 strand for Backstitch and French Knots. It was inserted in the lid of a 5" dia. porcelain jar (3½" dia. opening).

Butterfly and Daisy Pillow (shown on page 15): The design was stitched over 2 fabric threads on a 10" square of Ivory Lugana (25 ct). Three strands of floss were used for Cross Stitch and 1 strand for Backstitch and French Knots.

For pillow, center design and trim stitched piece to measure 6" dia. circle. You will also need 6" dia. circle of fabric for pillow backing, 5" x 54" strip of fabric for ruffle (pieced as necessary), 2" x 18" bias strip of coordinating fabric for cording, 18" length of ¼" dia. purchased cord, and polyester fiberfill.

Complete pillow following Pillow Finishing instructions, page 87.

Designed by Nancy Dockter.

flights of fancy

#1 (66w x 47h)

#2 (40w x 40h)

X	DMC	¼X	B'ST	X	DMC	¼X	B'ST
	310		◿	–	754		◻
▦	317	◢			780		◿
4	320	◿		▲	782		◿
■	351	◿	◿*	▨	783		◿
▬	351 &	◿		◨	797		◿
	356			★	798		◿
▨	352	◢		▨	799		◿
△ †	352 &	◿		○	800		◿
	353			◇	809		◻
☆	353			★	839		◿
	355		◿	◉	840		◿
◆	367	◿		✚	844		◿*
2	368	◻		▨	898		◿*
◇	402	◿		▨	921		◿★
■	413	◿		○	922		
▨	433	◿			935		◿★
	434	◿	◿*	▲	936		
◆	469	◿		▨	937		
▨	470	◿			938		◿
△	471	◿		◨	3031		
☆	472	◿		■	3371	◿	
	520		◿*	▨	3787		
V	645	◿		◻	3790		
X	646	◿			3799		◿
X	676	◿		●	310		French Knot
✳	725	◿		◉	844		French Knot
▨	726	◿					
▨	727	◽					
V	729	◿					
◉	744	◿					
✚	745	◻					

* Use 351 for butterfly in Design #2. Use 434 for letters in Design #1. Use 844 for butterfly in Design #1.

† Use 2 strands of first floss color listed and 1 strand of second floss color listed.

★ Use 520 for leaves and stems in Design #1. Use 921 for butterfly in Design #1. Use 935 for leaves in Design #2.

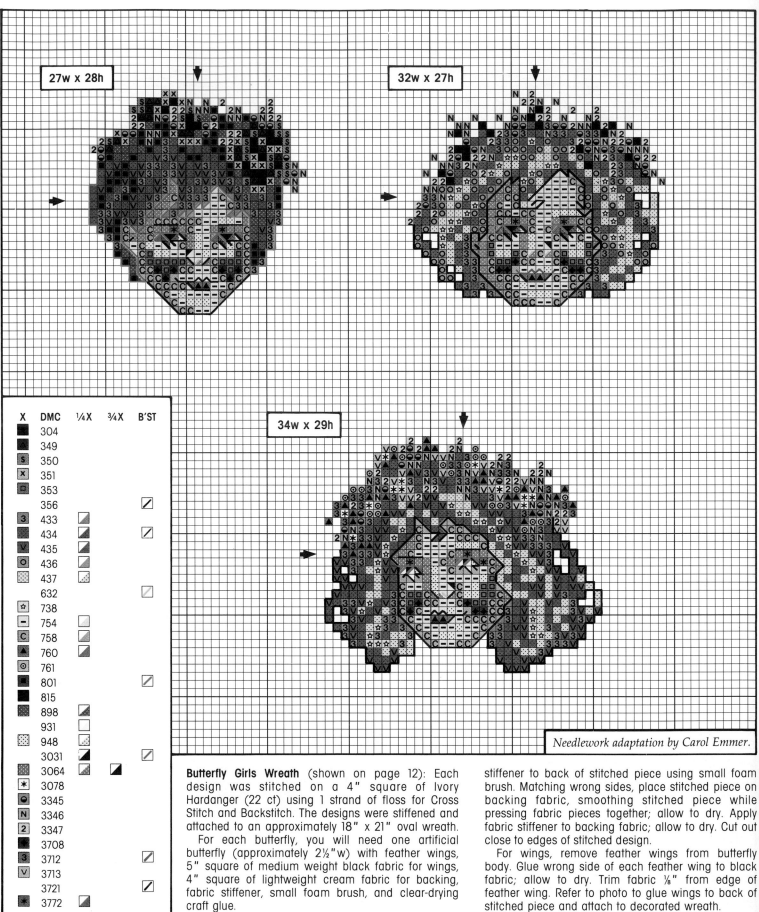

27w x 28h

32w x 27h

34w x 29h

X	DMC	1/4X	3/4X	B'ST
■	304			
▲	349			
S	350			
x	351			
□	353			
	356			╱
3	433	◢		╱
■	434	◢		╱
V	435	◢		
O	436	◢		
⦂	437	◢		
	632			╱
☆	738			
-	754	◢		
C	758	◢		
▲	760	◢		
⊙	761			
■	801			╱
■	815			
▨	898	◢		
	931	□		
⦂	948	◢		
▨	3031	◢		╱
▨	3064	◢	◢	
*	3078			
◉	3345			
N	3346			
2	3347			
■	3708			
3	3712			╱
V	3713			
	3721			╱
*	3772	◢		

Needlework adaptation by Carol Emmer.

Butterfly Girls Wreath (shown on page 12): Each design was stitched on a 4" square of Ivory Hardanger (22 ct) using 1 strand of floss for Cross Stitch and Backstitch. The designs were stiffened and attached to an approximately 18" x 21" oval wreath.

For each butterfly, you will need one artificial butterfly (approximately 2½"w) with feather wings, 5" square of medium weight black fabric for wings, 4" square of lightweight cream fabric for backing, fabric stiffener, small foam brush, and clear-drying craft glue.

For stiffened faces, apply a heavy coat of fabric stiffener to back of stitched piece using small foam brush. Matching wrong sides, place stitched piece on backing fabric, smoothing stitched piece while pressing fabric pieces together; allow to dry. Apply fabric stiffener to backing fabric; allow to dry. Cut out close to edges of stitched design.

For wings, remove feather wings from butterfly body. Glue wrong side of each feather wing to black fabric; allow to dry. Trim fabric ⅛" from edge of feather wing. Refer to photo to glue wings to back of stitched piece and attach to decorated wreath.

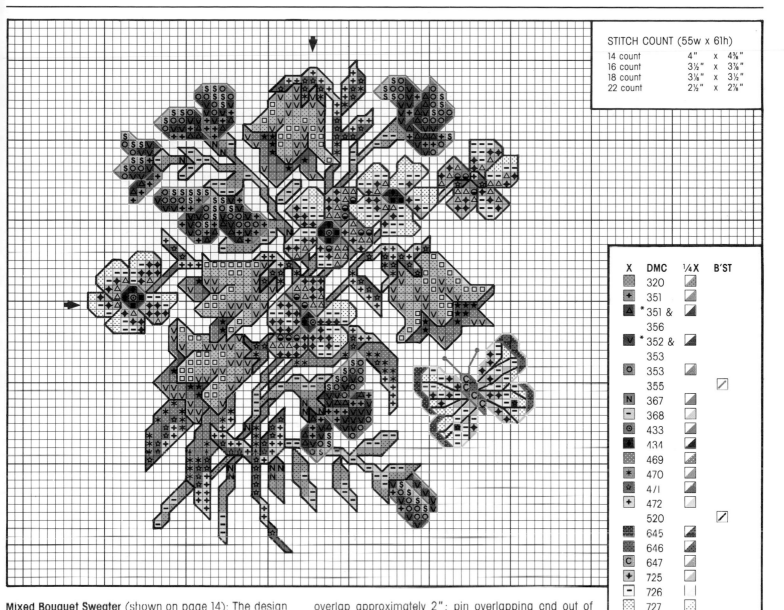

STITCH COUNT (55w x 61h)

14 count	4"	x	4⅜"
16 count	3½"	x	3⅞"
18 count	3⅛"	x	3½"
22 count	2½"	x	2⅞"

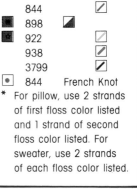

X	DMC	¼X	B'ST
■	320	◪	
+	351	◪	
▲	*351 & 356	◪	
V	*352 & 353	◪	
O	353	◪	
	355		/
N	367	◪	
-	368	◪	
⊙	433	◪	
■	434	◪	
■	469	◪	
✱	470	◪	
☆	471	◪	
+	472	◪	
	520		/
■	645	◪	
■	646	◪	
C	647	◪	
◆	725	◪	
-	726	◪	
░	727	◪	
S	754	◪	
	780		/
⊖	782	◪	/
△	783	◪	
★	797	◪	
■	798	◪	
V	799	◪	
□	800	◪	
░	809	◪	
	844		/
■	898	◪	
✩	922		/
	938		/
	3799		/
•	844	French Knot	

* For pillow, use 2 strands of first floss color listed and 1 strand of second floss color listed. For sweater, use 2 strands of each floss color listed.

Mixed Bouquet Sweater (shown on page 14): The design was stitched over a 10" square of 10 mesh waste canvas on a purchased sweater with top of design 1½" below bottom of neck band. Four strands of floss were used for Cross Stitch and 2 strands for Backstitch and French Knots. (See Working On Waste Canvas, page 62.)

Mixed Bouquet Pillow (shown on page 15): The design was stitched over 2 fabric threads on a 13" square of Ivory Lugana (25 ct) using 3 strands of floss for Cross Stitch and 1 strand for Backstitch and French Knots.

For pillow, center design and trim stitched piece to measure 8" square. You will also need an 8" square of fabric for backing, 6" x 64" strip of fabric for ruffle (pieced as necessary), 2" x 34" bias strip of coordinating fabric for cording, 34" length of ¼" dia. purchased cord, and polyester fiberfill.

Center cord on wrong side of bias strip; matching long edges, fold strip over cord. Use a zipper foot to baste along length of strip close to cord; trim seam allowance to ½". Matching raw edges, pin cording to right side of stitched piece making a ⅜" clip in seam allowance of cording at corners. Ends of cording should overlap approximately 2"; pin overlapping end out of the way. Starting 2" from beginning end of cording and ending 4" from overlapping end, baste cording to stitched piece. On overlapping end of cording, remove 2½" of basting; fold end of fabric back and trim cord so that it meets beginning end of cord. Fold end of fabric under ½"; wrap fabric over beginning end of cording. Finish basting cording to stitched piece.

For ruffle, press short edges of fabric strip ½" to wrong side. Matching wrong sides and long edges, fold strip in half; press. Machine baste ½" from raw edges, gather fabric strip to fit stitched piece. Matching raw edges, pin ruffle to right side of stitched piece overlapping short ends ¼". Use a ½" seam allowance to sew ruffle to stitched piece.

Matching right sides and leaving an opening for turning, use a ½" seam allowance to sew stitched piece and backing fabric together. Trim seam allowances diagonally at corners; turn pillow right side out carefully pushing corners outward. Stuff pillow with polyester fiberfill and blind stitch opening closed.

Designed by Nancy Dockter.

flights of fancy

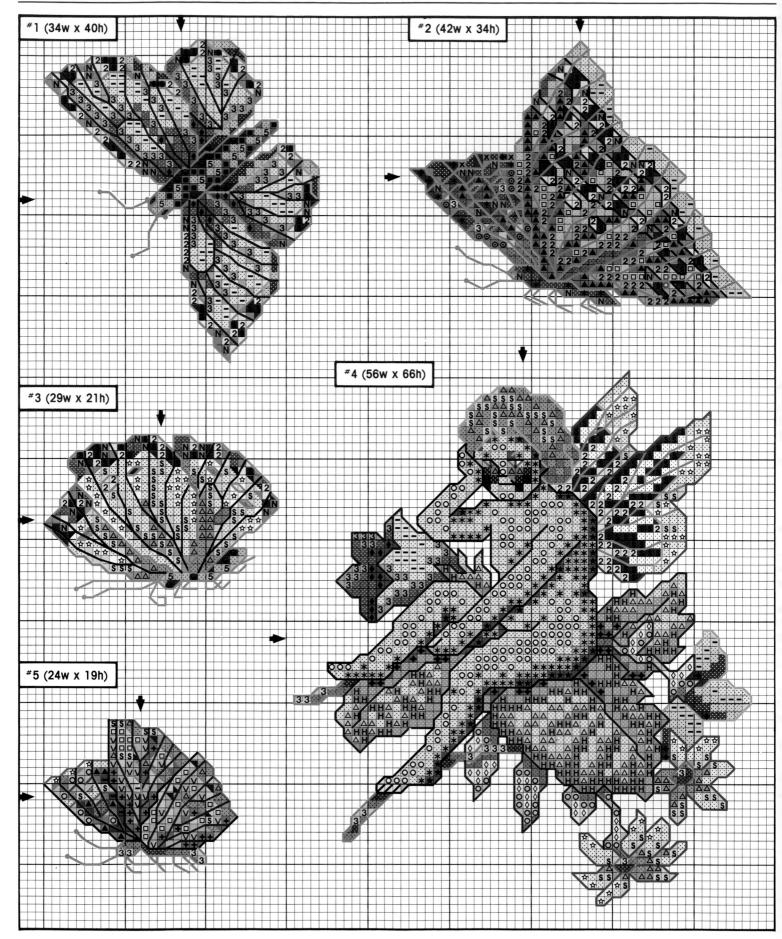

#1 (34w x 40h)

#2 (42w x 34h)

#3 (29w x 21h)

#4 (56w x 66h)

#5 (24w x 19h)

X	DMC	1/4X	3/4X	B'ST		X	DMC	1/4X	3/4X	B'ST		X	DMC	1/4X	3/4X	B'ST
	blanc	▨				▲	435	▨					869				◢ ♦
	310			◢ *		2	436	▨				◆	890	▨		
N	317	◨	◢	◢ *			437	▨					898	▨		
2	318	▨	◢				469	▨				◆	930	▨		
	319	◨				O	470	▨					931	▨		
△	320	◨				◊	471	▨				3	932	▨		
	351	◢		◢ †			520			◢ ▲		-	936	▨		◢
■★	351 &	◨				5	642	▨				▲	937	▨		
	356					S	676	▨	◨				938	▨		
	352	◢		◢ *			680	◨	◨	◢ †		O	948	▨		
-	353	▨				△	729	◨	◨	◢ ♦		■	3021	▨		
★	353 &	◨				□	739	▨				□	3348	▨		
	352						744	▨	◨			✚	3363	▨		
■★	353 &	◨				☆	745	▨	◨			V	3364	▨		
	760						754	▨				■	3371	▨		◢
	355			◢ ♦		*★	754 &	◨					3712		▨	
X	356	◢		◢ ▲		★	758					▨	3752	▨		
H	367	◢					758	▨				-	3753	▨		
	368	▨					760	◢				▨	3787	▨		
▨	413	◢	◢	◢ ▲		△	761	▨				✱	3799	▨		◢
▨	420	◨		◢			762	◢		◢		•	310	French Knot		
3	433	◨					798	▨		◢ †		•	3371	French Knot		
	434	▨				◎	801	◨								

* Use 310 for Designs #1, #2, and #3. Use 317 for Design #4. Use 352 for Design #5.

† Use 351 for Designs #3 and #5. Use 680 for wings and flowers in Design #4. Use 798 for eyes in Design #4.

★ For afghan, use 3 strands of each floss color listed. For sweater, use 2 strands of first floss color listed and 1 strand of second floss color listed.

♦ Use 355 for Design #1 and for flower in Design #4. Use 729 for wings in Design #4. Use 869 for hair and eyebrows in Design #4.

▲ Use 356 for Design #4. Use 413 for Designs #2 and #3. Use 520 for Design #5.

Butterflies and Fairy Afghan (shown on pages 10-11): Each design was stitched over 2 fabric threads on a 45" x 58" piece of Ivory Anne Cloth (18 ct).

For afghan, cut off selvages of fabric; measure 5½" from raw edge of fabric and pull out 1 fabric thread. Fringe fabric up to missing fabric thread. Repeat for each side. Tie an overhand knot at each corner with horizontal and 4 vertical fabric threads. Working from corners, use fabric threads for each knot until all threads are knotted.

Refer to Diagram for placement of designs on fabric; use 6 strands of floss for Cross Stitch, and 2 strands for Backstitch and French Knots.

For reins, thread a #24 tapestry needle with ⅛"w ribbon. Referring to photo for placement, carefully run ribbon through afghan fabric; tack in place as needed with matching sewing thread. Apply liquid fray preventative to ribbon ends.

Butterflies and Fairy Sweater (shown on page 13): Each design was stitched over a piece of 14 mesh waste canvas on a purchased sweater using 3 strands of floss for Cross Stitch and 1 strand for Backstitch and French Knots. Refer to photo for placement of designs. (See Working On Waste Canvas, page 62.)

For reins, thread a #24 tapestry needle with ⅛"w ribbon. Referring to photo for placement, carefully run ribbon through sweater fabric; tack in place as needed with matching sewing thread. Apply liquid fray preventative to ribbon ends.

Needlework adaptation by Nancy Dockter.

Diagram

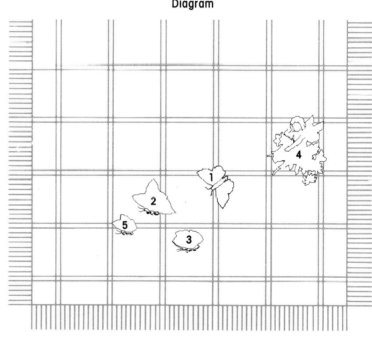

Violets So Fair

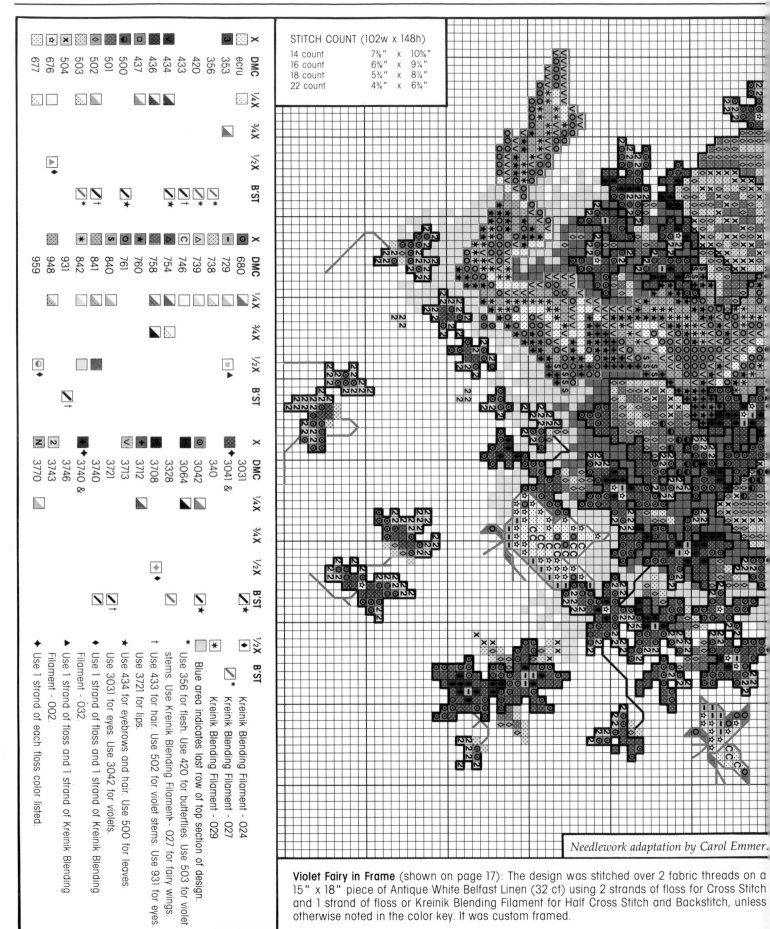

STITCH COUNT (102w x 148h)

14 count	7⅜"	x 10⅝"
16 count	6⅜"	x 9¼"
18 count	5¾"	x 8¼"
22 count	4¾"	x 6¾"

X	¼X	¾X	½X	B'ST	DMC
					3
					ecru
					353
					356
					420
					433
					434
					436
					437
					500
					501
					502
					503
					504
					676
					677

X	¼X	¾X	½X	B'ST	DMC
					680
					729
					738
					739
					746
					754
					758
					760
					761
					840
					841
					842
					931
					948
					959

X	¼X	¾X	½X	B'ST	DMC
					3031
					3041 &
					340
					3042
					3064
					3328
					3708
					3712
					3713
					3721
					3740
					3740 &
					3746
					3743
					3770

½X	B'ST	
		Kreinik Blending Filament - 024
		Kreinik Blending Filament - 027
		Kreinik Blending Filament - 029

* Blue area indicates last row of top section of design.
* Use 356 for flesh. Use 420 for butterflies and violet stems. Use Kreinik Blending Filament - 027 for fairy wings.
† Use 433 for hair. Use 502 for violet stems. Use 503 for violet stems.
† Use 3721 for lips.
★ Use 434 for eyebrows and hair. Use 500 for leaves.
Use 3031 for eyes. Use 3042 for violets.
◆ Use 1 strand of floss and 1 strand of Kreinik Blending Filament - 032.
◆ Use 1 strand of floss and 1 strand of Kreinik Blending Filament - 032.
▲ Use 1 strand of floss and 1 strand of Kreinik Blending Filament - 002.
◆ Use 1 strand of each floss color listed.

Needlework adaptation by Carol Emmer.

Violet Fairy in Frame (shown on page 17): The design was stitched over 2 fabric threads on a 15" x 18" piece of Antique White Belfast Linen (32 ct) using 2 strands of floss for Cross Stitch and 1 strand of floss or Kreinik Blending Filament for Half Cross Stitch and Backstitch, unless otherwise noted in the color key. It was custom framed.

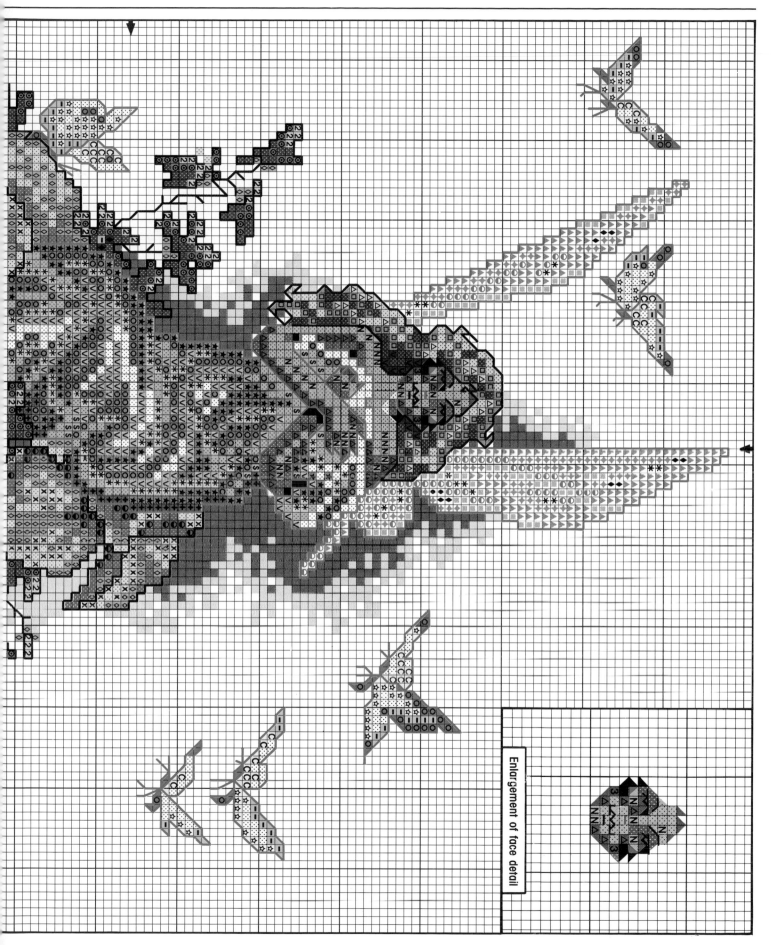

Enlargement of face detail

Violets So fair

#1

STITCH COUNT (96w x 96h)

14 count	6⅞"	x	6⅞"
16 count	6"	x	6"
18 count	5⅜"	x	5⅜"
22 count	4⅜"	x	4⅜"

Hath the pearl less whiteness
Because of its birth?
Hath the violet
less brightness
For growing
near earth?

Moore

#2 (30w x 30h)

#3 (30w x 30h)

MILL HILL BEADS

○	00221
+	00252
3	00332
-	02009
*	02011
C	03028
▨	03034

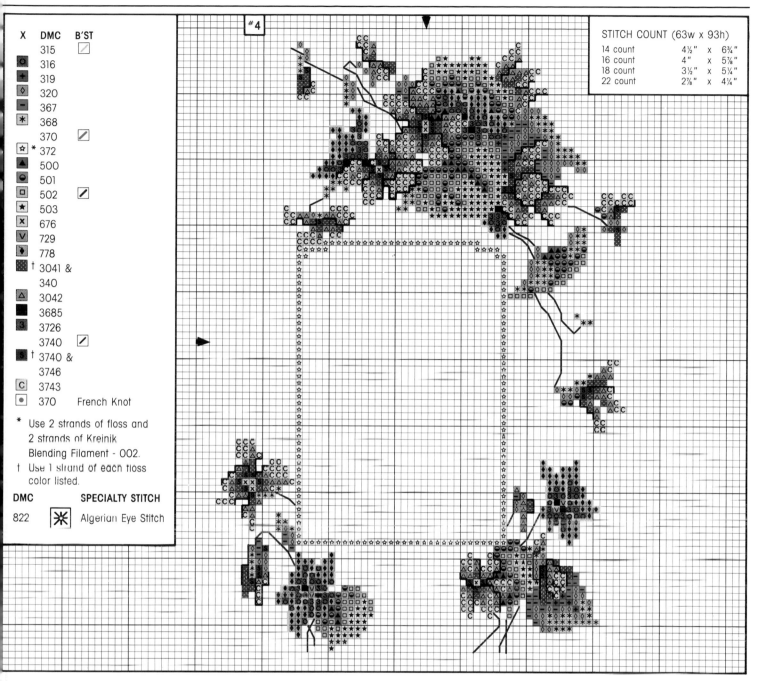

X	DMC	B'ST
	315	◹
◉	316	
✚	319	
◇	320	
▬	367	
✳	368	
	370	◹
☆ *	372	
▲	500	
◐	501	
◻	502	◹
★	503	
✕	676	
V	729	
◆	778	
⊡ †	3041 &	
	340	
△	3042	
■	3685	
⊠	3726	
	3740	◹
⬛ †	3740 &	
	3746	
C	3743	
⊙	370	French Knot

* Use 2 strands of floss and
 2 strands of Kreinik
 Blending Filament - 002.
† Use 1 strand of each floss
 color listed.

DMC	SPECIALTY STITCH
822	✳ Algerian Eye Stitch

STITCH COUNT (63w x 93h)

14 count	4½"	x	6¾"
16 count	4"	x	5⅞"
18 count	3½"	x	5¼"
22 count	2⅞"	x	4¼"

"Hath The Pearl" in Frame (shown on page 20): Design #1 was stitched over 2 fabric threads on a 14" square of Antique White Belfast Linen (32 ct) using 2 strands of floss for Cross Stitch and Algerian Eye Stitch, and 1 strand for Backstitch. Refer to Specialty Stitch Diagrams, page 82, for Algerian Eye Stitch. It was custom framed.

Beaded Sachets (shown on page 19): Designs #2 and #3 were each worked over 2 fabric threads on an 8" square of Antique White Belfast Linen (32 ct). To attach beads, use 1 strand of 822 DMC floss and refer to General Instructions, page 95.

For each sachet, center beaded design and trim fabric to measure 4" square. You will also need a 4" square of fabric for backing, 49" length of ¾"w flat lace, polyester fiberfill, and scented oil.

Press short ends of lace ½" to wrong side, machine baste ¼" from straight edge and gather lace to fit beaded design. Matching gathered edge of lace with raw edge of beaded design, baste lace to right side of beaded design.

Matching right sides and leaving an opening for turning, use a ¼" seam allowance to sew beaded design and backing fabric together. Trim seam allowances diagonally at corners; turn sachet right side out carefully pushing corners outward. Stuff sachet with polyester fiberfill; place a few drops of scented oil on a small amount of polyester fiberfill. Insert in middle of sachet and blind stitch opening closed.

Photo Mat in Frame (shown on page 18): Design #4 was stitched over 2 fabric threads on a 12" x 14" piece of Antique White Belfast Linen (32 ct) using 2 strands of floss for Cross Stitch and 1 strand for Backstitch, unless otherwise noted in the color key. It was custom framed.

To add photograph to stitched piece, you will need tracing paper, posterboard, rubber cement, and clear-drying craft glue. Cut a piece of posterboard same size as photograph; matching edges, use rubber cement to adhere posterboard to back of photograph. Use tracing paper to make a pattern of inside of cross-stitched border; cut out pattern. Position pattern over photograph as desired, draw around pattern and cut out along drawn line. Refer to photo and use craft glue to attach photograph to stitched piece.

Designed by Linda Culp Calhoun.

Violets So Fair

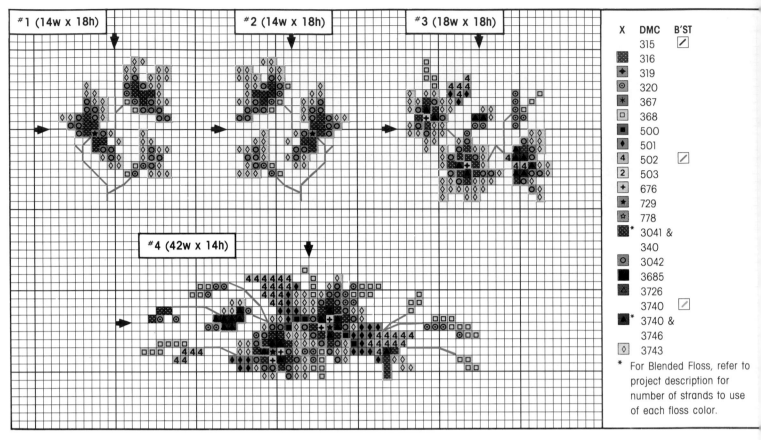

| | #1 (14w x 18h) | #2 (14w x 18h) | #3 (18w x 18h) | #4 (42w x 14h) |

X	DMC	B'ST
	315	✓
▦	316	
◆	319	
⊙	320	
✶	367	
▢	368	
■	500	
◆	501	
4	502	✓
2	503	
+	676	
★	729	
☆	778	
▦*	3041 &	
	340	
◉	3042	
■	3685	
▲	3726	
	3740	✓
■*	3740 &	
	3746	
◇	3743	

* For Blended Floss, refer to project description for number of strands to use of each floss color.

Violet Blouse (shown on page 20): Designs #1, #2, and #4 were stitched over 14 mesh waste canvas on a purchased blouse using 3 strands of floss for Cross Stitch and 1 strand for Backstitch. Designs #1 and #2 were stitched on the collar points and Design #4 was stitched on the pocket. For blended floss, use 2 strands of first floss color listed and 1 strand of second floss color listed.

Violet Handkerchief (shown on page 19): Design #3 was stitched over a 3" square of 14 mesh waste canvas on an 11½" square of handkerchief linen using 3 strands of floss for Cross Stitch and 1 strand for Backstitch. The design was stitched in one corner, 1" from edges of fabric. For blended floss, use 2 strands of first floss color listed and 1 strand of second floss color listed.

For handkerchief, you will need a 47" length of ¾"w pregathered lace.

Press short edges of lace ½" to wrong side. Matching bound edge of lace and raw edge of fabric, use ¼" seam allowance to sew lace to right side of fabric. Using a zigzag stitch, sew over raw edges to prevent fraying. Press seam allowances to wrong side of handkerchief. Use blind stitches to join pressed edges of lace.

Violet Sweater (shown on page 21): Design #5 was stitched over a 10" x 11" piece of 10 mesh waste canvas on a purchased sweater using 4 strands of floss for Cross Stitch and 2 strands for Backstitch. Refer to photo for placement of design. For blended floss, use 2 strands of each floss color listed.

Fringed Bookmark (shown on page 19): Design #6 was stitched over 2 fabric threads on an 8" x 12" piece of Antique White Belfast Linen (32 ct) using 2 strands for floss for Cross Stitch and 1 strand for Backstitch. For blended floss, use 1 strand of each floss color listed.

For bookmark, you will need blanc DMC Pearl Cotton #12. Work Nun Stitch ½" from edge of design on all sides; trim fabric close to Nun Stitch on long edges. Trim 1¾" from Nun Stitch on short edges; fringe to Nun Stitch. Refer to General Instructions, page 95, for Nun Stitch instructions.

Ribbon Bookmark (shown on page 19): Design #7 was stitched over 2 fabric threads on an 8" square of Antique White Belfast Linen (32 ct) using 2 strands for floss for Cross Stitch and 1 strand for Backstitch. For blended floss, use 1 strand of each floss color listed.

For bookmark, you will need blanc DMC Pearl Cotton #12, 13" length of 1"w ribbon, 13" length of ⅜"w ribbon, and thick clear-drying craft glue. Work Nun Stitch ¼" from edge of design on all sides; trim fabric close to Nun Stitch. Refer to General Instructions, page 95, for Nun Stitch instructions. Center and glue wrong side of ⅜"w ribbon to right side of 1"w ribbon; allow glue to dry. Fold one short edge 1½" to wrong side; glue in place. Trim remaining short edge diagonally. Refer to photo and glue stitched piece 1¼" from folded edge.

Designed by Linda Culp Calhoun.

WORKING ON WASTE CANVAS

Waste canvas is a special canvas the provides an evenweave grid for placin stitches on fabric. After the design is worke over the canvas, the canvas threads ar removed leaving the design on the fabric. Th canvas is available in several mesh sizes.

Cover edges of canvas with masking tape For sweater, cut a piece of lightweight, nor fusible interfacing the same size as canvas t provide a firm stitching base.

Find desired stitching area and mark cente of area with a pin. Match center of canvas t pin. Use the blue threads in canvas to plac canvas straight on project; pin canvas t project. (Pin interfacing to wrong side c sweater.) Baste all layers together as show in **Fig. 1**.

For sweater, place in a screw type hoop We recommend a hoop that is large enoug to encircle entire design.

Using a sharp needle, work desigr stitching from large holes to large holes. Tri canvas to within ¾" of design. Damper canvas until it becomes limp. Pull out canvc threads one at a time using tweezers (**Fig. 2** Trim interfacing close to design.

Fig. 1   **Fig. 2**

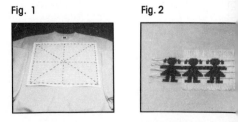

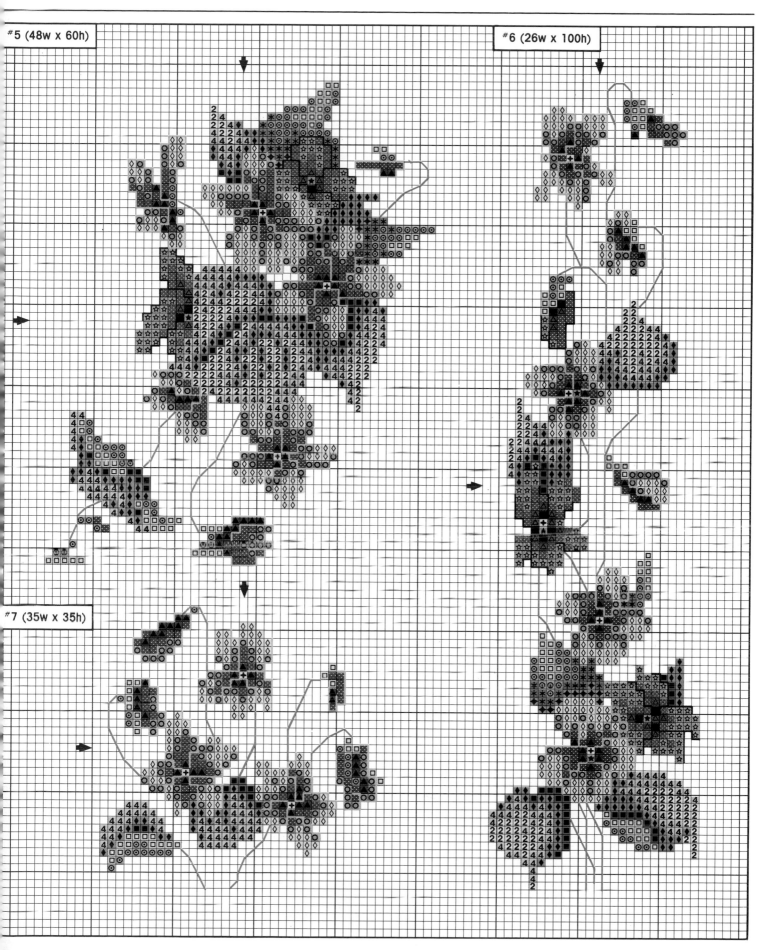

#5 (48w x 60h)

#6 (26w x 100h)

#7 (35w x 35h)

Blushing Rose

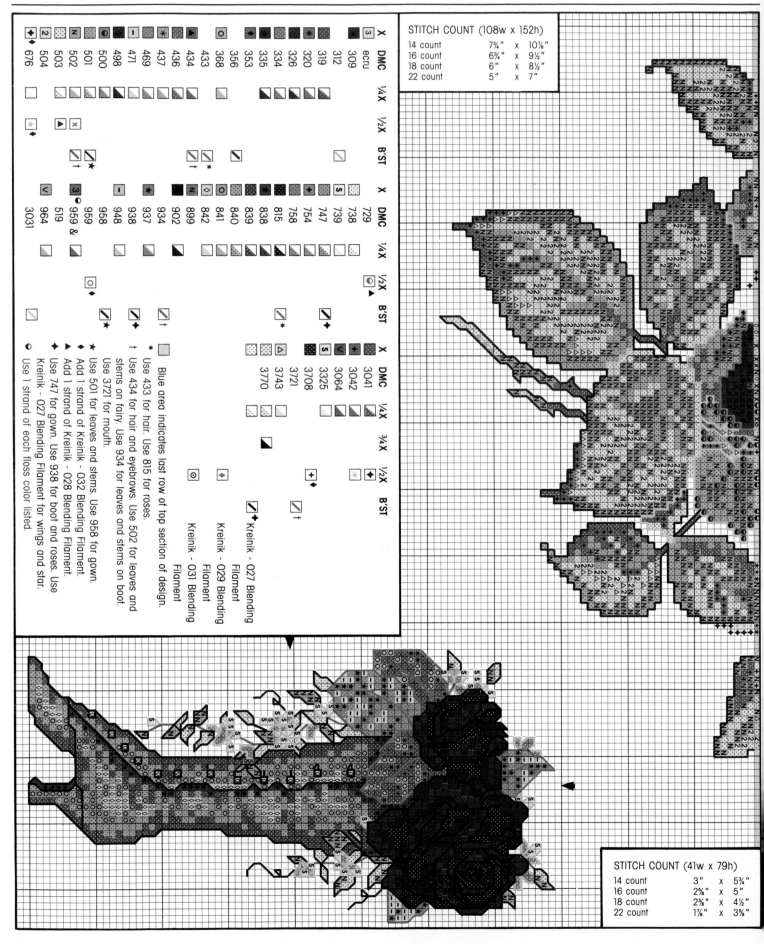

STITCH COUNT (108w x 152h)

14 count	7¾"	x	10⅞"
16 count	6¾"	x	9½"
18 count	6"	x	8½"
22 count	5"	x	7"

STITCH COUNT (41w x 79h)

14 count	3"	x	5¾"
16 count	2⅝"	x	5"
18 count	2⅜"	x	4½"
22 count	1⅞"	x	3⅝"

* Blue area indicates last row of top section of design.
* Use 433 for hair. Use 815 for roses.
† Use 434 for hair and eyebrows. Use 934 for leaves and stems on fairy. Use 502 for leaves and stems on boot.
Use 3721 for mouth.
Use 501 for leaves and stems. Use 958 for gown.
Add 1 strand of Kreinik - 032 Blending Filament.
Add 1 strand of Kreinik - 028 Blending Filament.
Use 747 for gown. Use 938 for boot and roses. Use Kreinik - 027 Blending Filament for wings and star. Use 1 strand of each floss color listed.

Enlargement of face detail

Victorian Boot Wall Pocket (shown on page 25): The design was stitched on a 9" x 11" piece of Cream Belfast Linen (32 ct) over 2 fabric threads using 2 strands of floss for Cross Stitch and 1 strand for Backstitch. (See Wall Pocket Finishing, page 68.)

Needlework adaptation by Jane Chandler.

Rose Fairy in Frame (shown on page 23): The design was stitched on an 18" x 15" piece of Cream Belfast Linen (32 ct) over 2 fabric threads using 2 strands of floss for Cross Stitch and 1 strand of floss or Kreinik Blending Filament for Half Cross Stitch and Backstitch, unless otherwise noted in the color key. It was custom framed.

Needlework adaptation by Carol Emmer.

Blushing Rose

#1 (71w x 42h)

#2 (77w x 78h)

#3 (78w x 78h)

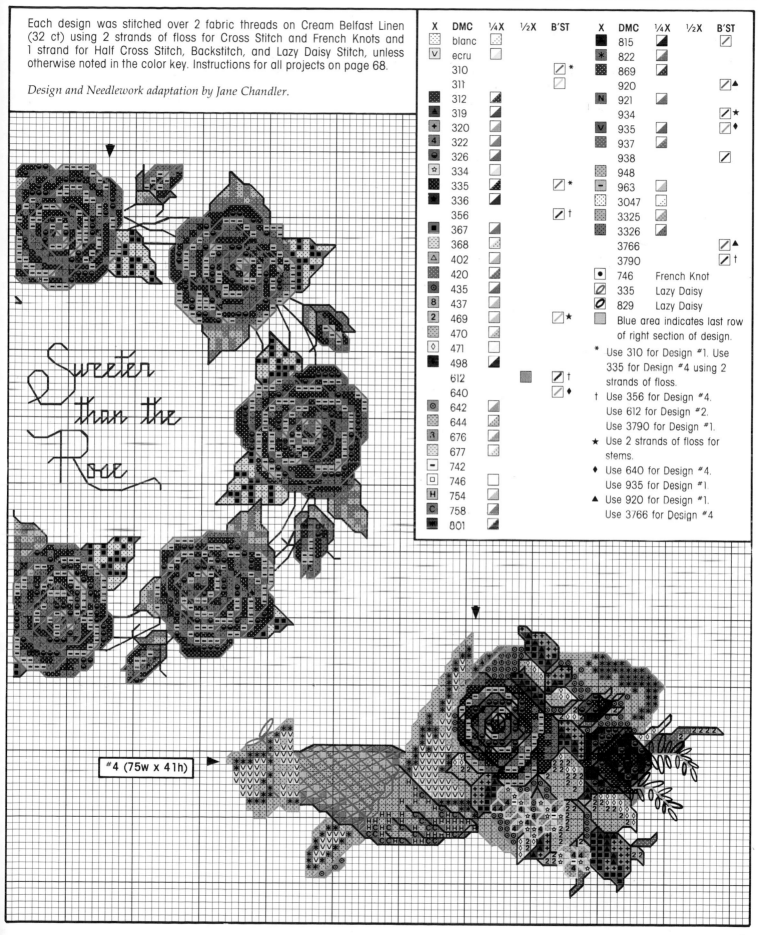

Each design was stitched over 2 fabric threads on Cream Belfast Linen (32 ct) using 2 strands of floss for Cross Stitch and French Knots and 1 strand for Half Cross Stitch, Backstitch, and Lazy Daisy Stitch, unless otherwise noted in the color key. Instructions for all projects on page 68.

Design and Needlework adaptation by Jane Chandler.

X	DMC	¼X	½X	B'ST
	blanc			
V	ecru			
	310			✓ *
	311			✓
	312			
	319			
	320			
	322			
	326			
	334			
	335			✓ *
	336			
	356			✓ †
	367			
	368			
	402			
	420			
	435			
	437			
	469			✓ ★
	470			
	471			
	498			
	612			✓ †
	640			✓ ♦
	642			
	644			
	676			
	677			
	742			
	746			
	754			
	758			
	801			

X	DMC	¼X	½X	B'ST
	815			✓
	822			
	869			
	920			✓ ▲
N	921			
	934			✓ ★
V	935			✓ ♦
	937			
	938			✓
	948			
-	963			
	3047			
	3325			
	3326			
	3766			✓ ▲
	3790			✓ †

• 746 French Knot
∅ 335 Lazy Daisy
∅ 829 Lazy Daisy

Blue area indicates last row of right section of design.

* Use 310 for Design #1. Use 335 for Design #4 using 2 strands of floss.

† Use 356 for Design #4. Use 612 for Design #2. Use 3790 for Design #1.

★ Use 2 strands of floss for stems.

♦ Use 640 for Design #4. Use 935 for Design #1.

▲ Use 920 for Design #1. Use 3766 for Design #4

#4 (75w x 41h)

Blushing Rose

Victorian Boxes (shown on pages 24-25, charts on pages 66-67): Designs #1, #3, and #4 were each stitched over 2 fabric threads on an 11" square of Cream Belfast Linen (32 ct) using 2 strands of floss for Cross Stitch and 1 strand for Backstitch and Lazy Daisy Stitches, unless otherwise noted in the color key.

Amounts of the following supplies will be determined by size of box.

For each Victorian box, you will need a Shaker box in desired shape and size, tracing paper for pattern of lid, batting for top of lid, fabric marking pencil, clear-drying craft glue, and assorted ribbons, trims, and decorative items.

VICTORIAN BOX FINISHING

Cut a tracing paper pattern ½" larger on all sides than box lid. Center pattern on stitched piece and pin pattern in place. Use fabric marking pencil to draw around pattern; remove pattern and cut out on drawn line. Clip ¼" into edge of stitched piece at 1" intervals. Cut batting same size as lid; glue batting on lid. Place stitched piece on batting; fold edge of stitched piece down and glue to side of lid. Refer to photo and glue ribbons, trims, and decorative items as desired.

Rose and Bud Porcelain Jar (shown on page 25, chart on pages 66-67): The top center rose and bud from Design #3 were stitched over 2 fabric threads on a 6" square of Cream Belfast Linen (32 ct) using 2 strands of floss for Cross Stitch and 1 strand for Backstitch, unless otherwise noted in the color key. It was inserted in the lid of a 3¾" x 2¾" oval porcelain jar (3" x 2" opening).

Victorian Boot Wall Pocket (shown on page 25, chart on page 64): The design was stitched over 2 fabric threads on a 9" x 11" piece of Cream Belfast Linen (32 ct) using 2 strands of floss for Cross Stitch and 1 strand for Backstitch.

For wall pocket, you will need a 9" x 11" piece of Belfast Linen for backing, two 9" x 11" pieces of fabric for lining, 13" length of ¼" dia. cording with attached seam allowance, 33" length of 1⅛"w flat lace, 11½" length of ¼"w ribbon, two 12" lengths of ⅛"w ribbon, four

Mill Hill Pebble Beads - 05147, tracing paper, and fabric marking pencil.

Trace Wall Pocket Pattern (page 96) onto tracing paper; cut out pattern. Referring to photo for placement, position pattern on wrong side of stitched piece and pin pattern in place. Use fabric marking pencil to draw around pattern, remove pattern and cut out on drawn line. Use pattern and cut **one** from backing fabric and **two** from lining fabric.

Matching right sides and leaving top edge open, use a ¼" seam allowance to sew stitched piece and backing fabric together; trim seam allowance diagonally at corners and turn wall pocket right side out carefully pushing corners outward.

Matching right sides and leaving top edge open, use a ⅜" seam allowance to sew lining fabric together; trim seam allowances close to stitching. **Do not turn lining right side out.** Press top edge of lining ¼" to wrong side.

If needed, trim seam allowance of cording to ¼". Beginning and ending at center back, match raw edges of wall pocket and cording. Start 1" from end of cording and baste cording to right side of wall pocket. Ends of cording should overlap 2"; turn overlapped ends of cording toward seam allowance and baste across overlapped ends.

Press short edges of lace ½" to wrong side and machine baste ¼" from straight edge; gather lace to fit top edge of wall pocket. Matching gathered edge of lace and raw edge of wall pocket, baste lace to right side of wall pocket. Use a zipper foot and a ¼" seam allowance sew lace and cording to wall pocket; press seam allowance to wrong side. With wrong sides facing, place lining inside wall pocket; blind stitch in place. For hanger, refer to photo and blind stitch one end of ¼"w ribbon to inside of each side seam.

For streamers, place one pebble bead on each end of both lengths of ⅛"w ribbon, knot ribbon ¾" from each end to hold beads; trim ends as desired. Refer to photo and align lengths of ribbon as desired and tie in an overhand knot; tack streamers to right side seam.

Design and needlework adaptation by Jane Chandler.

Rose Basket Pillow (shown on page 24, chart on page 66): Design #2 was stitched over 2 fabric threads on a 13" square of Cream Belfast Linen (32 ct) using 2 strands of floss for Cross Stitch and 1 strand for Half Cross Stitch, Backstitch, and French Knots.

For pillow, center design and trim stitched piece to measure 9" square. You will also need a 9" square of fabric for pillow backing, 5½" x 64" strip of fabric for ruffle (pieced as necessary), 64" length of 2½"w flat lace, 2" x 38" bias strip of fabric for cording, 38" length of ¼" dia. purchased cord, and polyester fiberfill.

Center cord on wrong side of bias strip; matching long edges, fold strip over cord. Use a zipper foot to baste along length of strip close to cord; trim seam allowance to ½". Matching raw edges, pin cording to right side of stitched piece making a ⅜" clip in seam allowance of cording at corners. Ends of cording should overlap approximately 2"; pin overlapping end out of the way. Starting 2" from beginning end of cording and ending 4" from overlapping end, baste cording to stitched piece. On overlapping end of cording, remove 2½" of basting; fold end of fabric back and trim cord so that it meets beginning end of cord. Fold end of fabric under ½"; wrap fabric over beginning end of cording. Finish basting cording to stitched piece.

For fabric and lace ruffle, press short edges of fabric strip ½" to wrong side. Matching wrong sides and long edges, fold strip in half; press. Press short edges of lace ½" to wrong side. Matching raw edges of fabric strip and straight edge of lace, machine baste layers together ½" from raw edges; gather to fit stitched piece. Matching raw edges, pin ruffle to right side of stitched piece overlapping short edges ¼". Use a ½" seam allowance to sew ruffle to stitched piece.

Matching right sides and leaving an opening for turning, use a ½" seam allowance to sew stitched piece and backing fabric together. Trim seam allowances diagonally at corners; turn pillow right side out carefully pushing corners outward. Stuff pillow with polyester fiberfill and blind stitch opening closed.

Needlework adaptation by Nancy Dockter.

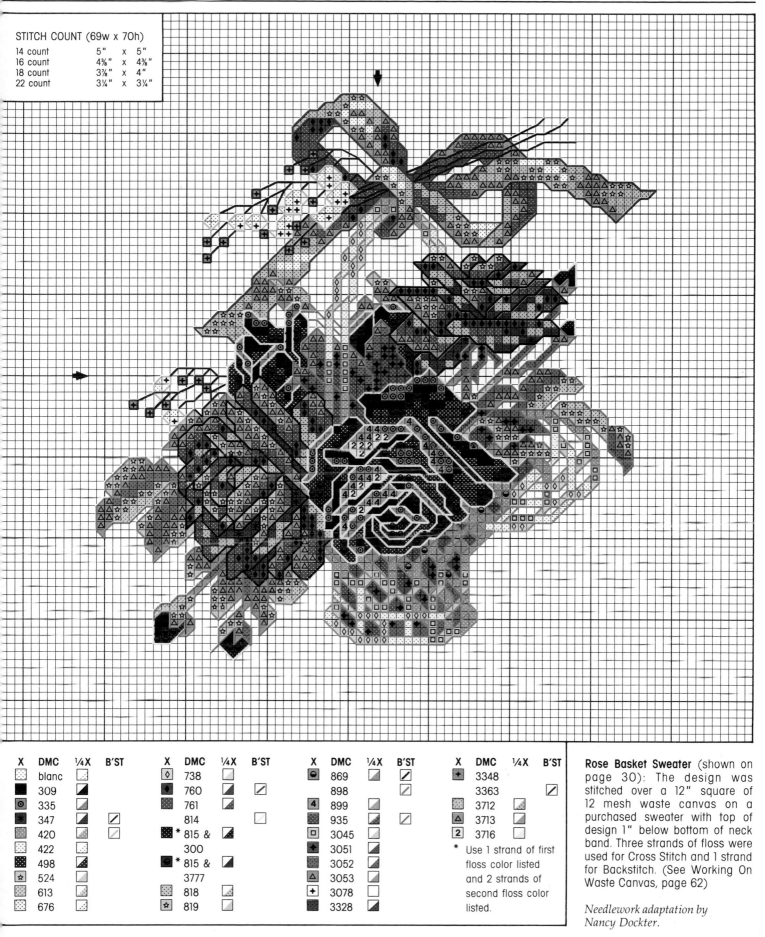

STITCH COUNT (69w x 70h)

14 count	5"	x	5"
16 count	4⅜"	x	4⅜"
18 count	3⅞"	x	4"
22 count	3¼"	x	3¼"

X	DMC	¼X	B'ST		X	DMC	¼X	B'ST		X	DMC	¼X	B'ST		X	DMC	¼X	B'ST		X	DMC	¼X	B'ST
	blanc				◇	738				◉	869		✓		✚	3348		
■	309				◆	760		✓			898		✓			3363		✓
⊙	335					761				4	899					3712		
✳	347		✓			814					935		✓		△	3713		
	420		✓		■	*815 &				▫	3045				2	3716		
	422					300				✦	3051							
	498				◉	*815 &					3052				* Use 1 strand of first			
☆	524					3777				△	3053				floss color listed			
	613					818				✚	3078				and 2 strands of			
	676				★	819					3328				second floss color			
															listed.			

Rose Basket Sweater (shown on page 30): The design was stitched over a 12" square of 12 mesh waste canvas on a purchased sweater with top of design 1" below bottom of neck band. Three strands of floss were used for Cross Stitch and 1 strand for Backstitch. (See Working On Waste Canvas, page 62)

Needlework adaptation by Nancy Dockter.

Gather Ye Rosebuds

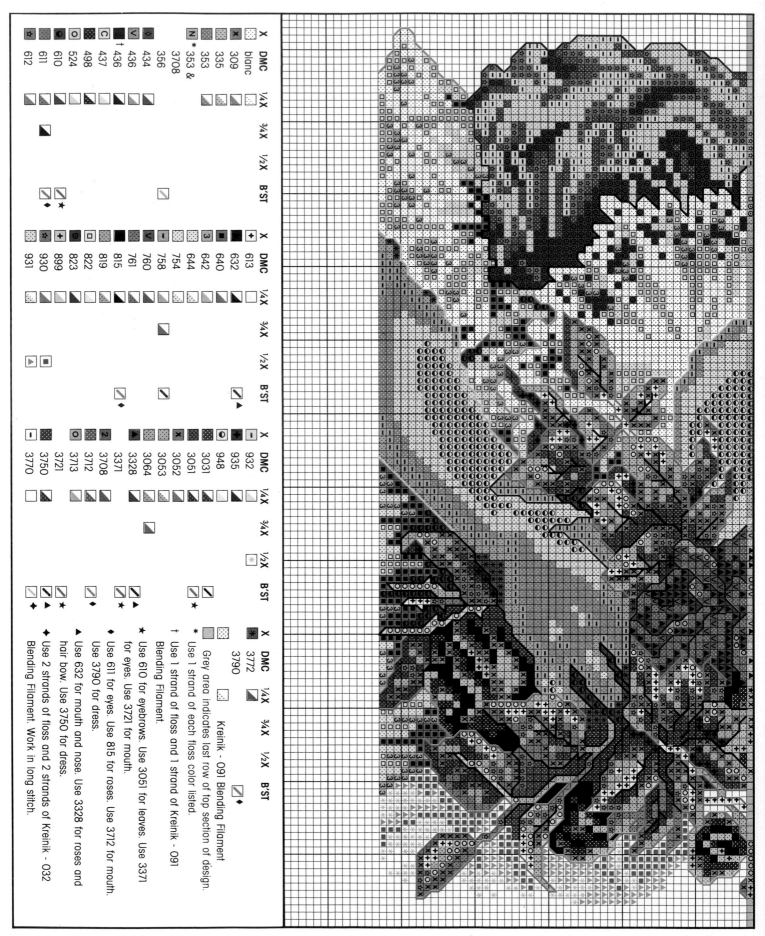

X	DMC	¼X	¾X	½X	B'ST
	blanc				
x	309				
	335				
	353				
N *	353 & 3708				
	356				
◊	434				
V	436				
†	436				
C	437				
	498				
O	524				
	610				★
	611				♦
☆	612				
+	613				
	632				▲
	640				
3	642				
	644				
	754				
-	758				
V	760				
	761				
	815				♦
	819				
□	822				
	823				
+	899				
☆	930				
	931				
-	932				
	935				
	948				
	3031				
	3051				★
x	3052				
	3053				
	3064				
▲	3328				▲
	3371				★
2	3708				
	3712				♦
O	3713				
	3721				★
	3750				▲
-	3770				✦
*	3772				
	3790				♦

Kreinik - 091 Blending Filament

Grey area indicates last row of top section of design.

* Use 1 strand of each floss color listed.

† Use 1 strand of floss and 1 strand of Kreinik - 091 Blending Filament.

★ Use 610 for eyebrows. Use 3051 for leaves. Use 3371 for eyes. Use 3721 for mouth.

♦ Use 611 for eyes. Use 815 for roses. Use 3712 for mouth. Use 3790 for dress.

▲ Use 632 for mouth and nose. Use 3328 for roses and hair bow. Use 3750 for dress.

✦ Use 2 strands of floss and 2 strands of Kreinik - 032 Blending Filament. Work in long stitch.

STITCH COUNT (122w x 137h)			
14 count	8¾"	x	9⅞"
16 count	7⅝"	x	8⅝"
18 count	6⅞"	x	7⅝"
22 count	5⅝"	x	6¼"

Sweeter Than The Rose in Frame (shown on page 26): The design was stitched over 2 fabric threads on a 16" x 17" piece of Cream Belfast Linen (32 ct) using 2 strands of floss or Kreinik Blending Filament for Cross Stitch and 1 strand of floss for Half Cross Stitch and Backstitch, unless otherwise noted in the color key. It was custom framed.

Needlework adaptation by Carol Emmer.

STITCH COUNT (75w x 104h)

14 count	5⅜"	x	7½"
16 count	4¾"	x	6½"
18 count	4¼"	x	5⅞"
22 count	3½"	x	4¾"

Gather ye rosebuds while ye may, Old time is still a-flying; And this same flower that smiles today, Tomorrow will be dying.

HERRICK

"Gather Ye Rosebuds" in Frame (shown on page 32): The design was stitched over 2 fabric threads on a 13" x 15" piece of Cream Belfast Linen (32 ct) using 2 strands of floss for Cross Stitch and 1 strand for Backstitch. It was custom framed.

Needlework adaptation by Nancy Dockter.

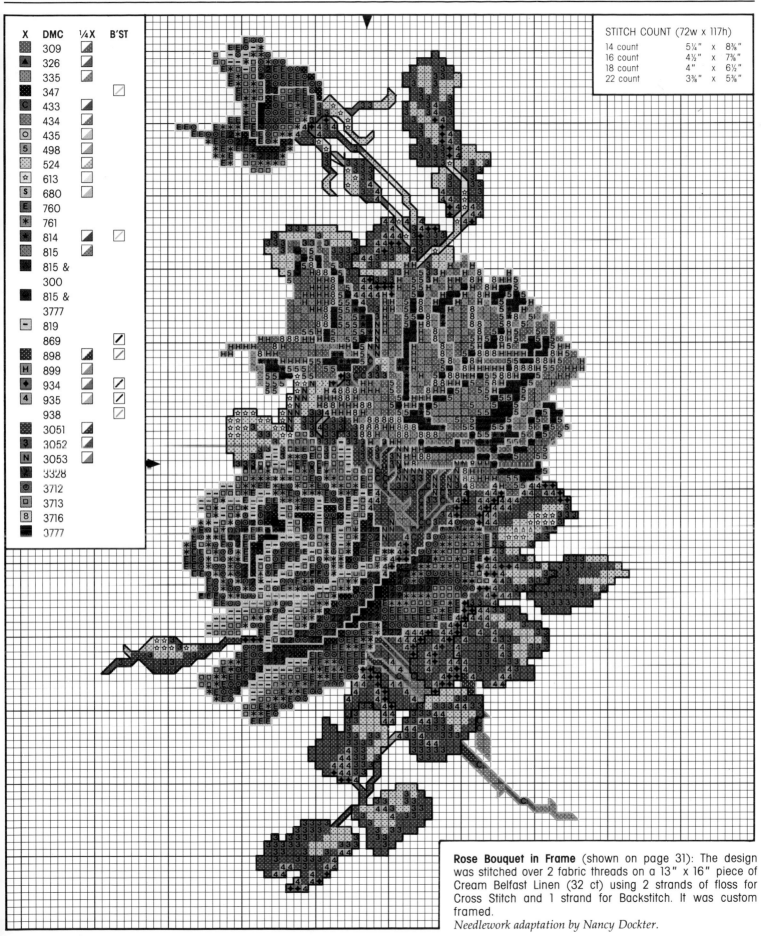

X	DMC	¼X	B'ST
	309		
▲	326		
	335		
	347		
C	433		
	434		
O	435		
5	498		
	524		
☆	613		
S	680		
E	760		
*	761		
✱	814		
	815		
	815 & 300		
	815 & 3777		
-	819		
	869		
	898		
H	899		
◆	934		
4	935		
	938		
	3051		
3	3052		
N	3053		
	3328		
◎	3712		
□	3713		
8	3716		
	3777		

STITCH COUNT (72w x 117h)

14 count	5¼"	x	8⅜"
16 count	4½"	x	7⅜"
18 count	4"	x	6½"
22 count	3⅜"	x	5⅜"

Rose Bouquet in Frame (shown on page 31): The design was stitched over 2 fabric threads on a 13" x 16" piece of Cream Belfast Linen (32 ct) using 2 strands of floss for Cross Stitch and 1 strand for Backstitch. It was custom framed.

Needlework adaptation by Nancy Dockter.

Gather Ye Rosebuds

Rose Afghan (shown on page 29): Each design was stitched over 2 fabric threads on a 45" x 58" piece of Ivory Anne Cloth (18 ct) using 6 strands of floss for Cross Stitch and 2 strands for Backstitch. Refer to Diagram for placement of designs on fabric. Use a zigzag stitch to sew over raw edges to prevent fraying.

For afghan, you will need a 45" x 58" piece of fabric for backing, 2⅞ yards of fabric for ruffle, and 5⅛ yard length of 1⅛"w flat lace.

For ruffle, piece fabric as necessary to make a 10" x 11 yard strip of fabric. Press short edges of fabric strip ½" to wrong side. Matching wrong sides and long edges fold strip in half; press. Machine baste ½" from raw edges, gather fabric strip to fit around outside edge of afghan.

Matching raw edges and beginning at bottom center, pin ruffle to right side of afghan. Use a ½" seam allowance to machine baste ruffle to afghan. Use blind stitches to join pressed short edges of ruffle.

Matching right sides and leaving an opening for turning, use a ½" seam allowance to sew afghan and backing fabric together. Trim seam allowances diagonally at corners and turn afghan right side out carefully pushing corners outward. Blind stitch opening closed.

Refer to photo for placement of lace and pin along edge of afghan, folding lace to form a mitered corner at each corner. Machine sew inside edge of lace to afghan through all layers. Tack outside edge of lace to afghan.

Diagram

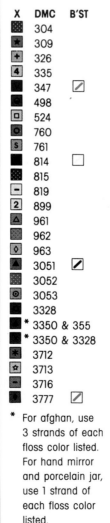

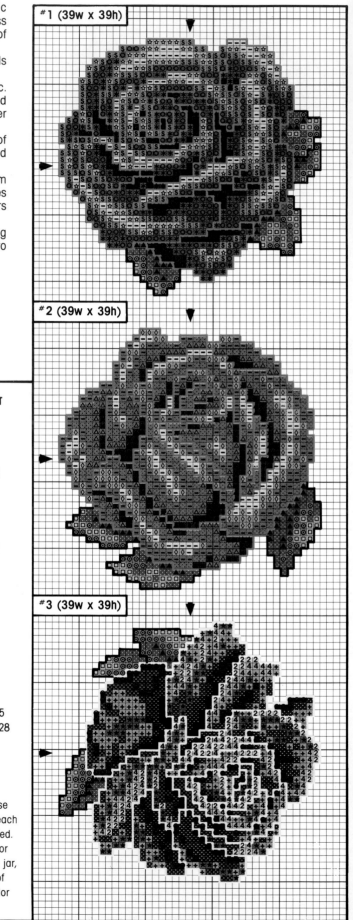

X	DMC	B'ST
▓	304	
★	309	
✦	326	
4	335	
■	347	╱
◪	498	
□	524	
◎	760	
S	761	
■	814	╱
▨	815	
–	819	
2	899	
▲	961	
▨	962	
◇	963	
▲	3051	╱
▨	3052	
◉	3053	
■	3328	
■	* 3350 & 355	
■	* 3350 & 3328	
✱	3712	
☆	3713	
▬	3716	
■	3777	╱

* For afghan, use 3 strands of each floss color listed. For hand mirror and porcelain jar, use 1 strand of each floss color listed.

Rose Hand Mirror (shown on page 30): Design #1 was stitched over 2 fabric threads on an 8" square of Cream Belfast Linen (32 ct) using 2 strands of floss for Cross Stitch and 1 strand for Backstitch. It was inserted in a wooden hand mirror (3½" dia. opening).

Rose Porcelain Jar (shown on page 28): Design #2 was stitched over 2 fabric threads on an 8" square of Cream Belfast Linen (32 ct) using 2 strands of floss for Cross Stitch and 1 strand for Backstitch. It was inserted in the lid of a 5" dia. porcelain jar (3½" dia. opening).

Designed by Nancy Dockter

74

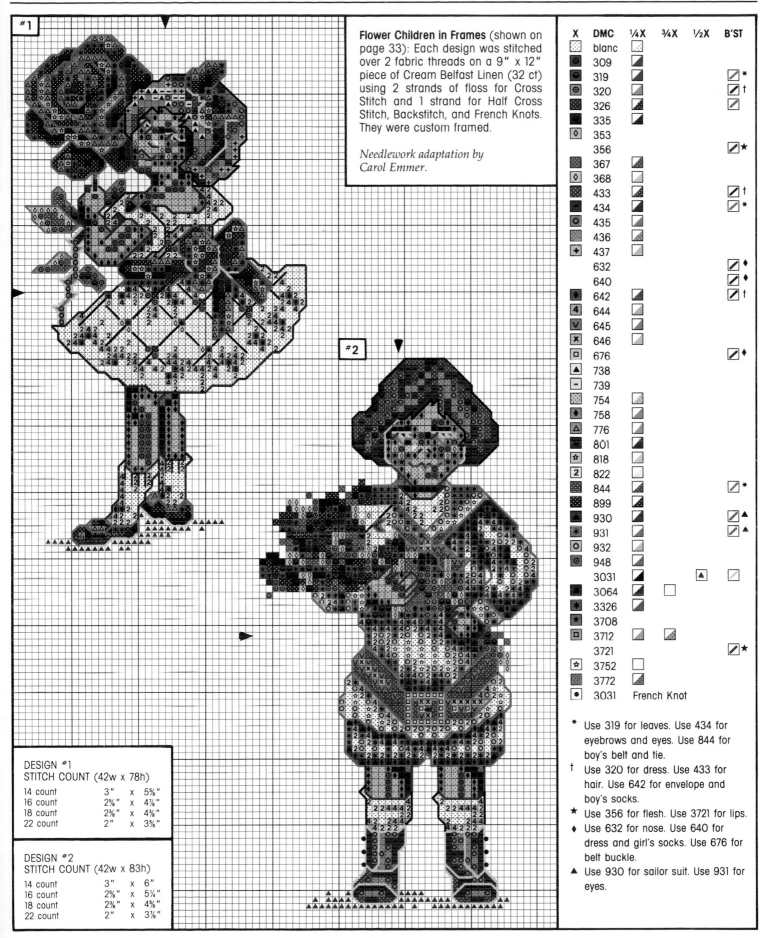

Flower Children in Frames (shown on page 33): Each design was stitched over 2 fabric threads on a 9" x 12" piece of Cream Belfast Linen (32 ct) using 2 strands of floss for Cross Stitch and 1 strand for Half Cross Stitch, Backstitch, and French Knots. They were custom framed.

Needlework adaptation by Carol Emmer.

X	DMC	¼X	¾X	½X	B'ST
	blanc				
	309				
	319				✓ *
	320				✓ †
	326				✓
	335				
	353				
	356				✓ ★
	367				
	368				
	433				✓ †
	434				✓ *
	435				
	436				
	437				
	632				✓ ♦
	640				✓ ♦
	642				✓ †
4	644				
V	645				
X	646				
	676				✓ ♦
▲	738				
–	739				
	754				
	758				
△	776				
	801				
☆	818				
2	822				
	844				✓ *
	899				
✳	930				✓ ▲
✳	931				✓ ▲
	932				
	948				
	3031			▲	✓
	3064		□		
	3326				
★	3708				
	3712				
	3721				✓ ★
☆	3752				
	3772				
●	3031	French Knot			

* Use 319 for leaves. Use 434 for eyebrows and eyes. Use 844 for boy's belt and tie.

† Use 320 for dress. Use 433 for hair. Use 642 for envelope and boy's socks.

★ Use 356 for flesh. Use 3721 for lips.

♦ Use 632 for nose. Use 640 for dress and girl's socks. Use 676 for belt buckle.

▲ Use 930 for sailor suit. Use 931 for eyes.

DESIGN #1
STITCH COUNT (42w x 78h)

14 count	3"	x	5⅝"
16 count	2⅝"	x	4⅞"
18 count	2⅜"	x	4⅜"
22 count	2"	x	3⅝"

DESIGN #2
STITCH COUNT (42w x 83h)

14 count	3"	x	6"
16 count	2⅝"	x	5¼"
18 count	2⅜"	x	4⅝"
22 count	2"	x	3⅞"

Samplers in Bloom

Rose Sampler in Frame (shown on page 35): The design was stitched over 2 fabric threads on a 14" x 20" piece of Cream Belfast Linen (32 ct) using 2 strands of floss for Cross Stitch and 1 strand for Backstitch and French Knots, unless otherwise noted in the color key. Refer to chart for type of thread and number of strands used for Specialty Stitches (refer to Specialty Stitch Diagrams, pages 82-83). It was custom framed.

Designed by Linda Culp Calhoun.

STITCH COUNT (96w x 190h)		
14 count	6⅞"	x	13⅝"
16 count	6"	x	11⅞"
18 count	5⅜"	x	10⅝"
22 count	4⅜"	x	8¾"

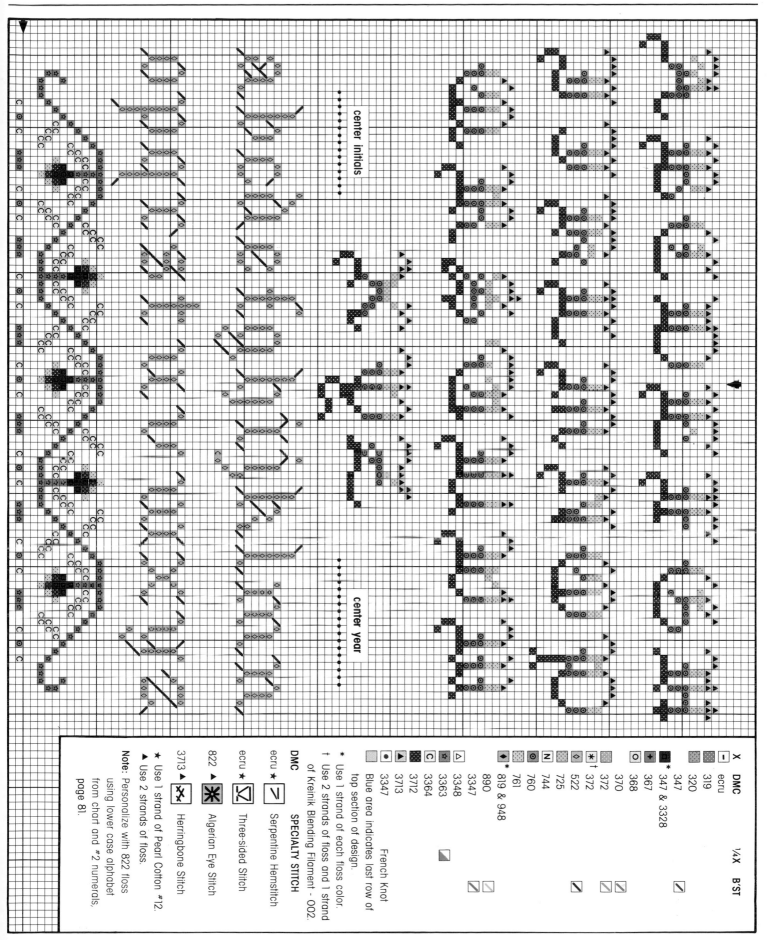

center initials

center year

Samplers in Bloom

72w x 130h

center initials

center year

X	DMC	B'ST	X	DMC	B'ST
▲	208		C	553	
+	209		□	554	
	210			642	╱
−	211			644	╱
S	368			725	
x	369		⊙	726	
⊖	500	╱	*	727	
	501		N	782	╱
V	502		x	822	╱
◇	503			3078	
✳	520	╱	−	3348	
O	522		+	3363	
▨	550		2	3364	
✦	552	╱	○	Mill Hill Bead - 03021	

DMC		SPECIALTY STITCH
822 *	✳	Algerian Eye Stitch
822 & 211 †	✳	Double Cross Stitch
ecru ★	☐	Four-sided Stitch
369 *	⋈	Herringbone Stitch
ecru ★	—	Interlacing
211 *	⋙	Montenegrin Stitch
ecru ★	⦀	Pins Stitch
ecru ♦	⦀	Satin Stitch
ecru ★	╱	Serpentine Hemstitch

* Use 2 strands of floss.
† Use 1 strand of 822 floss for large Cross Stitch. Use 1 strand of 211 floss for Upright Cross.
★ Use 1 strand of Pearl Cotton #12.
♦ Use 1 strand of Pearl Cotton #8.

Note: Personalize Violet Sampler with 822 floss using alphabet from chart and #2 numerals, page 81.

Note: Personalize Pansy Sampler with 642 floss using #1 alphabet and #3 numerals, page 81.

Violet Sampler and Pansy Sampler in Frames (shown on pages 36-37): Each design was stitched over 2 fabric threads on a 12" x 16" piece of Cream Belfast Linen (32 ct) using 2 strands of floss for Cross Stitch and 1 strand for Backstitch. Refer to chart for type of thread and number of strands used for Specialty Stitches (refer to Specialty Stitch Diagrams, pages 82-83). To attach beads, use 1 strand of 822 DMC floss and refer to General Instructions, page 95. They were custom framed.

Designed by Linda Culp Calhoun.

the sweetest rose will
wither, the violets will
depart, but oh the
lovely pansies – they
live within my heart,

center name and year

Samplers in Bloom

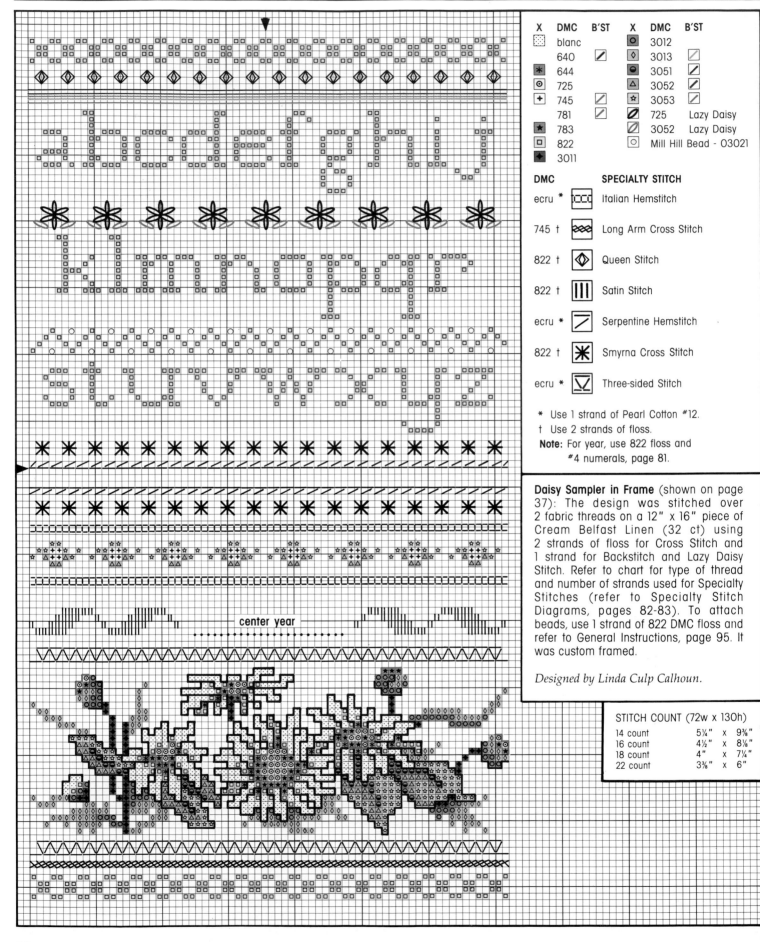

X	DMC	B'ST	X	DMC	B'ST
⬚	blanc		◉	3012	/
	640	/	◇	3013	/
✱	644		⊖	3051	/
◉	725		△	3052	/
✚	745	/	☆	3053	/
	781	/	⬤	725	Lazy Daisy
★	783		⬤	3052	Lazy Daisy
⬜	822		◎	Mill Hill Bead - 03021	
◆	3011				

DMC		SPECIALTY STITCH
ecru *	⬚⬚⬚	Italian Hemstitch
745 †	⧓	Long Arm Cross Stitch
822 †	◇	Queen Stitch
822 †	‖‖‖	Satin Stitch
ecru *	/	Serpentine Hemstitch
822 †	✳	Smyrna Cross Stitch
ecru *	▽	Three-sided Stitch

* Use 1 strand of Pearl Cotton #12.
† Use 2 strands of floss.
Note: For year, use 822 floss and #4 numerals, page 81.

center year

Daisy Sampler in Frame (shown on page 37): The design was stitched over 2 fabric threads on a 12" x 16" piece of Cream Belfast Linen (32 ct) using 2 strands of floss for Cross Stitch and 1 strand for Backstitch and Lazy Daisy Stitch. Refer to chart for type of thread and number of strands used for Specialty Stitches (refer to Specialty Stitch Diagrams, pages 82-83). To attach beads, use 1 strand of 822 DMC floss and refer to General Instructions, page 95. It was custom framed.

Designed by Linda Culp Calhoun.

STITCH COUNT (72w x 130h)		
14 count	5¼"	x 9⅜"
16 count	4½"	x 8⅛"
18 count	4"	x 7¼"
22 count	3⅜"	x 6"

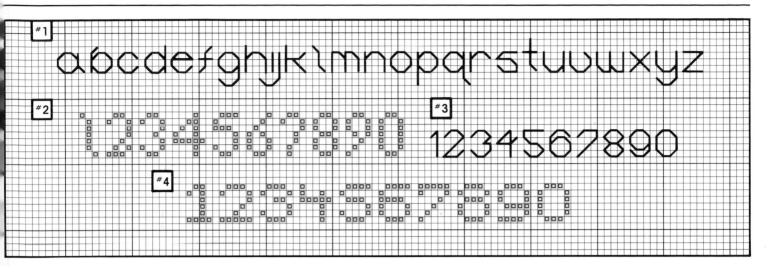

Sachet Bags (shown on page 39): Portions (refer to photo) of the Violet Sampler and Pansy Sampler (charts on pages 78-79) were each stitched over 2 fabric threads on a 6" square of Cream Belfast Linen (32 ct) with bottom of design 1" from one edge. Use 2 strands of floss for Cross Stitch and 1 strand for Backstitch. Refer to chart for type of thread and number of strands for Specialty Stitches (refer to Specialty Stitch Diagrams, pages 82-83). To attach beads, use 1 strand of 822 DMC floss and refer to General Instructions, page 95.

For each sachet bag, trim fabric ¾" from design on side edges and 2" from design on top edge. You will also need a piece of Belfast Linen same size as stitched piece for backing, 18" length of ⅝"w flat lace, 18" length of ⅛"w ribbon, polyester fiberfill, and scented oil.

Matching right sides and leaving top edge open, use a ¼" seam allowance to sew stitched piece and backing fabric together; trim seam allowances diagonally at corners. Turn top edge of bag ¼" to wrong side and press; turn ¼" to wrong side again and hem. Press short edges of lace ½" to wrong side and machine baste close to straight edge; gather lace to fit top edge of bag. Refer to photo to blind stitch gathered edge of lace to wrong side of top edge of bag. Turn bag right side out and stuff bag with polyester fiberfill. Place a few drops of scented oil on a small amount of fiberfill and insert in middle of bag. Tie ribbon in a bow around bag; trim ends as desired.

Hanging Sachet Pillows (shown on page 39): Portions (refer to photo) of the Violet Sampler and Pansy Sampler (charts on pages 78-79) were each stitched over 2 fabric threads on a 5" square of Cream Belfast Linen (32 ct) using 2 strands of floss for Cross Stitch and 1 strand for Backstitch.

For each pillow, center design and trim stitched piece to measure 2½" x 2¾". You will also need a 2½" x 2¾" piece of Belfast Linen for backing, 24" length of ⅞"w flat lace, two 14" lengths of ⅛"w ribbon, polyester fiberfill, and scented oil.

Press short edges of lace ½" to wrong side, machine baste ¼" from straight edge and gather lace to fit stitched piece. Matching gathered edge of lace with raw edge of fabric, baste lace to right side of stitched piece.

Matching right sides and leaving an opening for turning, use a ¼" seam allowance to sew stitched piece and backing fabric together. Trim seam allowances diagonally at corners, turn sachet right side out carefully pushing corners outward. Stuff sachet with polyester fiberfill; place a few drops of scented oil on a small amount of polyester fiberfill and insert in middle of sachet and blind stitch opening closed. Refer to photo to tack one length of ribbon to each upper corner of pillow, trim ends as desired.

Floral Towels (shown on page 38): The floral band and Specialty Stitch above and below the floral band from the Violet Sampler, Pansy Sampler and Daisy Sampler (charts on pages 78-80) were each stitched over 2 fabric threads across one short end of a 13½" x 19" piece of Cream Bantry Cloth (28 ct). Center each design horizontally with bottom of design 1⅝" from short edge. Referring to photo, extend Specialty Stitch to edges of fabric. Two strands of floss were used for Cross Stitch and 1 strand for Backstitch. Refer to chart for type of thread and number of strands used for Specialty Stitches (refer to Specialty Stitch Diagrams, pages 82-83).

For each towel, you will need a 34" length of 1⅝"w flat lace.

Press short edges of lace ½" to wrong side and machine baste ¼" from straight edge; gather lace to fit short edge of fabric. On cross stitched end, match gathered edge of lace to raw edge of fabric and use a ¼" seam allowance to sew lace to right side of fabric. Using a zigzag stitch to prevent fraying, sew close to seam; trim close to zigzag stitch. Press seam allowance to wrong side of towel. For remaining raw edge, turn fabric ¼" to wrong side and press; turn ¼" to wrong side again and hem.

Basket Cloth (shown on page 39): The small flowers and beads from the Violet Sampler (chart on page 78) were stitched over 2 fabric threads on a 21" square of Cream Belfast Linen (32 ct) with bottom of design 1¾" from raw edge of fabric on all sides. Use 2 strands of floss for Cross Stitch. To attach beads, use 1 strand of 822 DMC floss and refer to General Instructions, page 95.

For basket cloth, you will need 822 DMC Pearl Cotton #12. Work Nun Stitch 1" from edge of fabric on all sides; trim close to Nun Stitch. Refer to General Instructions, page 95, for Nun Stitch instructions.

Designed by Linda Culp Calhoun.

SPECIALTY STITCH DIAGRAMS

(**Note:** For Figs. with numbered stitches, come up at 1 and all odd numbers; go down at 2 and all even numbers.)

PULLED STITCHES

When working Pulled Stitches, fabric threads should be pulled tightly together to create an opening in the fabric around the stitch. Figs. show placement of stitch but do not show pulling of the fabric threads. Keep tension even throughout work.

Algerian Eye Stitch: An "eye" is formed in the center of this stitch. Come up at 1, go down in center, and pull tightly toward 3. Come up at 3, go down in center, and pull tightly toward 5; continue working in this manner until stitch is complete (stitches 5-15) (**Fig. 1**). Work row of Algerian Eye Stitches from right to left.

Fig. 1

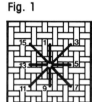

Four-sided Stitch: This continuous stitch is worked from left to right. Come up at 1 and pull tightly toward 2; then go down at 2 and pull tightly toward 1. Work stitches 3-14 in same manner (**Fig. 2**). Continue working in the same manner to end of row.

Fig. 2

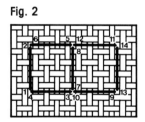

Pins Stitch: This stitch is a series of straight stitches worked side by side (**Fig. 3**). Complete stitch 1-2, come up at 3, and pull tightly; go down at 4, come up at 5, and pull tightly. Continue working in the same manner to end of row.

Fig. 3

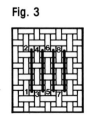

Three-sided Stitch: This continuous stitch is worked from right to left. Each stitch is worked twice; stitches 1-2 and 3-4 are over the same fabric threads (**Fig. 4a**). Come up at 1 and pull tightly toward 2; then go down at 2 and pull tightly toward 1. Work stitch 3-4 over the same fabric threads. Work stitches 5-22 in same manner (**Figs. 4a-c**). Continue working in the same manner to end of row.

Fig. 4a   **Fig. 4b**

          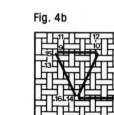

Fig. 4c

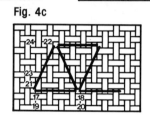

DRAWN THREAD STITCHES

When working Drawn Thread Stitches, horizontal fabric threads are first withdrawn from a section of fabric. The remaining vertical threads are pulled together into groups to form an open, patterned effect. The number of threads withdrawn (given in the individual stitch instructions) is determined by the stitch being worked.

At center of area to be withdrawn, carefully cut horizontal fabric threads one at a time. Withdraw each fabric thread by using a needle to unweave the thread one intersection at a time to edges of design (**Fig. 5a**). Thread needle with end of withdrawn fabric thread. Reweave thread into fabric for approximately ½" (**Fig. 5b**), keeping rewoven edge straight (**Fig. 5c**). On back of fabric, cut end of rewoven thread close to fabric. When beginning or ending a drawn thread stitch, weave pearl cotton through rewoven area to secure.

Fig. 5a   **Fig. 5b**

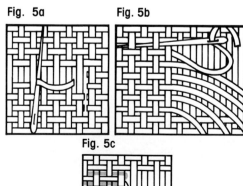

Fig. 5c

Interlacing: This stitch twists groups of threads together for a lacy effect. Withdraw and reweave eight fabric threads (**Figs. 5a-c**). Work from left to right with groups of six threads. Insert needle from front to back of fabric, six threads from rewoven edge; catch last three threads and bring needle back to front (**Fig. 6a**). Twist point of needle to back and around to front (**Fig. 6b**), catching first three threads. Continue in the same manner across withdrawn area.

Fig. 6a   **Fig. 6b**

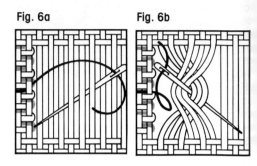

Italian Hemstitch: This stitch is worked in two withdrawn areas that are two fabric threads apart. Withdraw and reweave one fabric thread. Leaving two fabric threads woven, withdraw and reweave one more fabric thread (**Figs. 5a-c**). Working from right to left, come up at 1; take needle down at 2, coming up at 1 to catch two threads as shown in **Fig. 7a**. Take needle down at 3, coming up at 4 to catch two threads (**Fig. 7b**). Take needle down at 3, come up at 5 (**Fig. 7c**), and pull tightly. Continue in the same manner across withdrawn area (**Fig. 7d**).

Fig. 7a   **Fig. 7b**

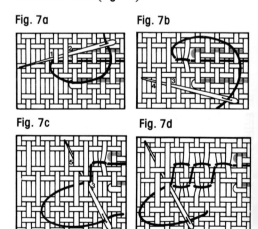

Fig. 7c   **Fig. 7d**

Serpentine Hemstitch: This stitch is worked across both edges of a withdrawn area. Withdraw and reweave six fabric threads (**Figs. 5a-c**). Working from left to right, come up at 1; take needle down at 2, coming up at 3 to catch four threads as shown in **Fig. 8a**. Take needle down at 2, come up at 4 (**Fig. 8b**), and pull tightly. Continue in the same manner across lower edge of withdrawn area. Turn stitched piece upside down. Working from left to right, come up at 1; take needle down at 2, coming up at 3 to catch two threads as shown in **Fig. 8c**. Take needle down at 2, come up at 4 (**Fig. 8d**), and pull tightly. Take needle down at 5, coming up at 6 to catch four threads as shown in **Fig. 8e**. Take needle down at 5, come up at 7 (**Fig. 8e**), and pull tightly. Continue in the same manner across withdrawn area, catching groups of four threads (two from each group worked on opposite edge). The last group will be only two threads.

Fig. 8a

Fig. 8b

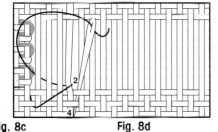

Fig. 8c   **Fig. 8d**

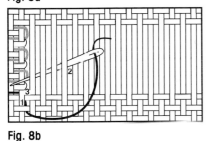

Fig. 8e

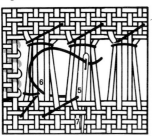

EMBROIDERY STITCHES

Double Cross Stitch: This decorative stitch is worked as a continuous stitch. Work large Cross Stitch (stitches 1-4) as shown in **Fig. 9a**; Then work Upright Cross (stitches 5-8) over center of large Cross Stitch (**Fig. 9b**). The top stitch of the Upright Cross must be made in the same direction on all Double Cross Stitches worked.

Fig. 9a   **Fig. 9b**

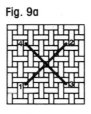
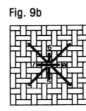

Herringbone Stitch: This overlapping stitch is worked continuously from left to right. Complete first stitch (stitches 1-4); then work next stitch (stitches 5-8) as shown in **Fig. 10**. Work all consecutive stitches in the same manner as stitches 5-8.

Fig. 10

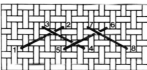

Long Arm Cross Stitch: This overlapping stitch is worked continuously from left to right. Complete first stitch (stitches 1-4); then work next stitch (stitches 5-8) as shown in **Fig. 11**. Work all consecutive stitches in the same manner as stitches 5-8.

Fig. 11

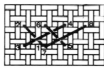

Montenegrin Stitch: This overlapping stitch is worked continuously from left to right. Complete first stitch (stitches 1-6) as shown in **Fig. 12a**; then work next stitch (stitches 7-12) (**Fig. 12b**). Work all consecutive stitches in the same manner as stitches 7-12.

Fig. 12a   **Fig. 12b**

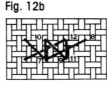

Queen Stitch: This decorative stitch forms a diamond shape. Work a long stitch (stitch 1-2) loosely and catch with a short stitch (stitch 3-4) (**Fig. 13a**). Complete stitch (stitches 5-16), catching each long stitch with a short stitch as shown in **Figs. 13a-c**.

Fig. 13a   **Fig. 13b**   **Fig. 13c**

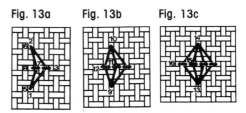

Rice Stitch: This decorative stitch is formed by first working a large Cross Stitch (stitches 1-4) and then working a stitch over each leg of the Cross Stitch (stitches 5-12) as shown in **Fig. 14**.

Fig. 14

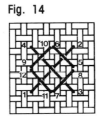

Satin Stitch: This stitch is a series of straight stitches worked side by side (**Fig. 15**). The number of threads worked over and the direction of stitches will vary according to the chart.

Fig. 15

Smyrna Cross Stitch: This decorative stitch is formed by working four stitches (stitches 1-8) as shown in **Fig. 16**. The top stitch (stitch 7-8) of all Smyrna Cross Stitches must be made in the same direction.

Fig. 16

Pansy Potpourri

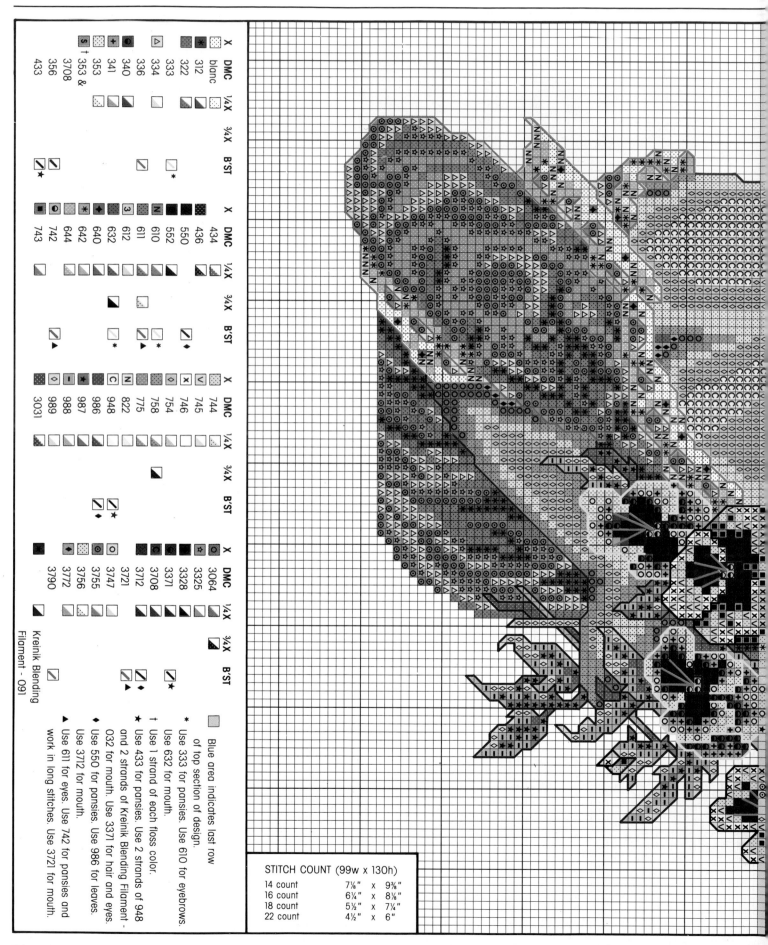

Blue area indicates last row of top section of design.

* Use 333 for pansies. Use 610 for eyebrows.
  Use 632 for mouth.
† Use 1 strand of each floss color.
★ Use 433 for pansies. Use 2 strands of 948 and 2 strands of Kreinik Blending Filament - 032 for mouth. Use 3371 for hair and eyes.
◆ Use 550 for pansies. Use 986 for leaves.
◆ Use 3712 for mouth.
▶ Use 611 for eyes. Use 742 for pansies and work in long stitches. Use 3721 for mouth.

Kreinik Blending Filament - 091

STITCH COUNT (99w x 130h)		
14 count	7⅛"	x 9⅜"
16 count	6¼"	x 8⅛"
18 count	5½"	x 7¼"
22 count	4½"	x 6"

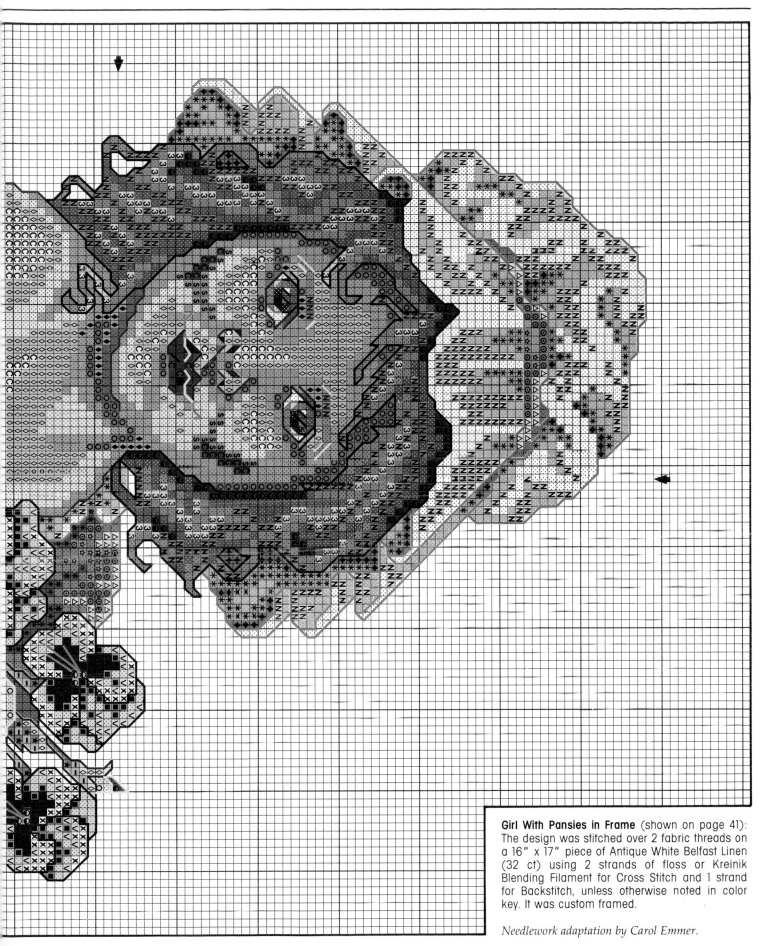

Girl With Pansies in Frame (shown on page 41): The design was stitched over 2 fabric threads on a 16" x 17" piece of Antique White Belfast Linen (32 ct) using 2 strands of floss or Kreinik Blending Filament for Cross Stitch and 1 strand for Backstitch, unless otherwise noted in color key. It was custom framed.

Needlework adaptation by Carol Emmer.

pansy potpourri

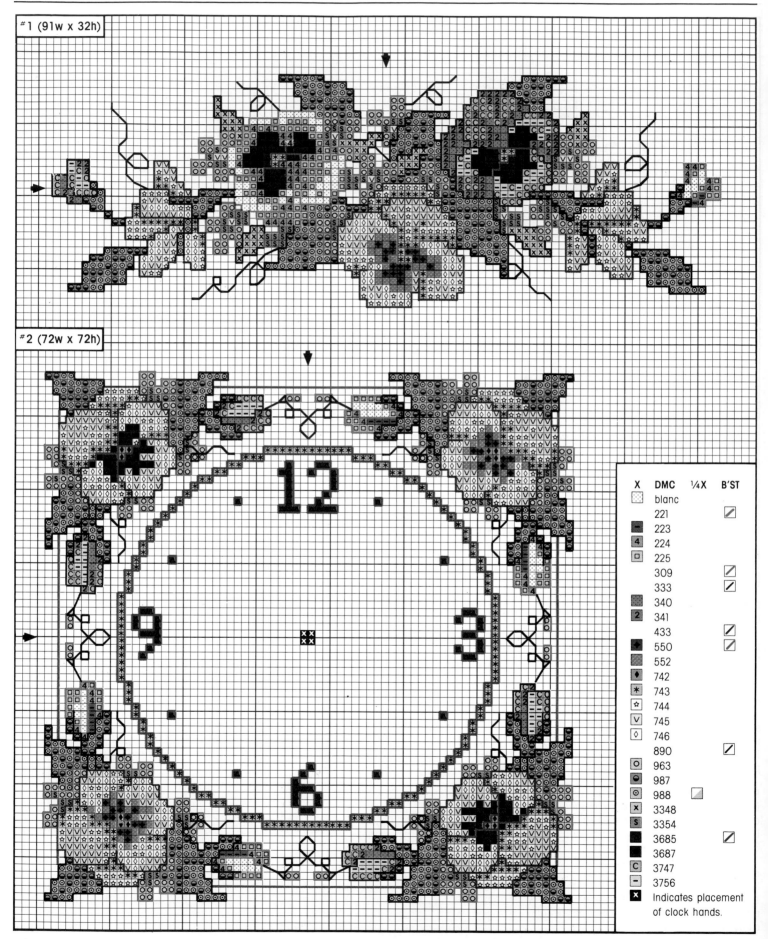

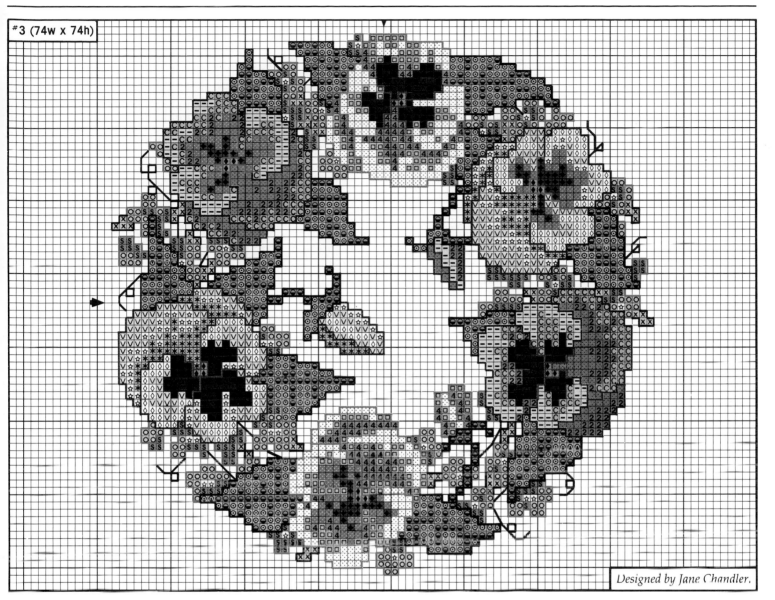

Designed by Jane Chandler.

Pansy Pillowcases (shown on page 42): Design #1 was stitched over a 12" x 7" piece of 12 mesh waste canvas, centered on the band of a pillowcase using 3 strands of floss for Cross Stitch and 1 strand for Backstitch. (See Working On Waste Canvas, page 62.)

Pansy Clock (shown on page 43): Design #2 was stitched over 2 fabric threads on a 10" square of Antique White Belfast Linen (32 ct) using 2 strands of floss for Cross Stitch and 1 strand for Backstitch. It was inserted in a purchased clock (5" square opening).

Pansy Shaker Box (shown on page 40): Design #3 was stitched over 2 fabric threads on an 11" square of Antique White Belfast Linen (32 ct) using 2 strands of floss for Cross Stitch and 1 strand for Backstitch.

For Shaker box, you will need a 6" dia. round Shaker box, tracing paper for pattern of lid, batting for top of lid, 19½" length of 1½"w pregathered lace, 12" length of ¼"w ribbon for bow, fabric marking pencil, and clear-drying craft glue.

Complete Shaker box following Victorian Box Finishing instructions, page 68.

Pansy Wreath Pillow (shown on page 42): Design #3 was stitched over 2 fabric threads on a 14" square of Antique White Lugana (25 ct) using 3 strands of floss for Cross Stitch and 1 strand for Backstitch.

For pillow, center design and trim stitched piece to measure 9½" dia. circle. You will also need a 9½" dia. circle of fabric for backing, 5" x 90" strip of fabric for ruffle (pieced as necessary), 2" x 29" bias strip of coordinating fabric for cording, 29" length of ¼" dia. purchased cord, and polyester fiberfill.

PILLOW FINISHING
Center cord on wrong side of bias strip; matching long edges, fold strip over cord. Use a zipper foot to baste along length of strip close to cord; trim seam allowance to ½". Matching raw edges, pin cording to right side of stitched piece. Ends of cording should overlap approximately 2"; pin overlapping end out of the way. Starting 2" from beginning end of cording and ending 4" from overlapping end, baste cording to stitched piece. On overlapping end of cording, remove 2½" of basting; fold end of fabric back and trim cord so that it meets beginning end of cord. Fold end of fabric under ½"; wrap fabric over beginning end of cording. Finish basting cording to stitched piece.

For ruffle, press short edges of fabric strip ½" to wrong side. Matching wrong sides and long edges, fold strip in half; press. Machine baste ½" from raw edges, gather fabric strip to fit stitched piece. Matching raw edges, pin ruffle to right side of stitched piece overlapping short ends ¼". Use a ½" seam allowance to sew ruffle to stitched piece.

Matching right sides and leaving an opening for turning, use a ½" seam allowance to sew stitched piece and backing fabric together. Trim seam allowances to ¼" and clip curves as needed; turn pillow right side out. Stuff pillow with polyester fiberfill and blind stitch opening closed.

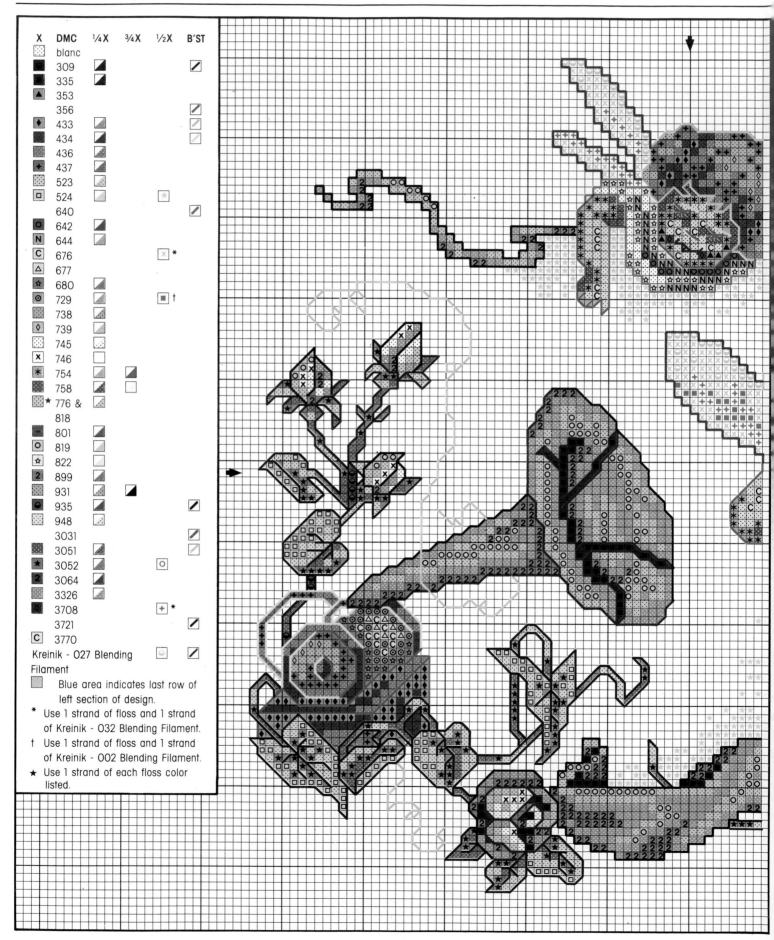

X	DMC	¼X	¾X	½X	B'ST
	blanc				
	309				
	335				
	353				
	356				
	433				
	434				
	436				
	437				
	523				
	524				
	640				
	642				
N	644				
C	676				*
	677				
	680				
	729				†
	738				
	739				
	745				
x	746				
	754				
	758				
★	776 &				
	818				
	801				
	819				
	822				
2	899				
	931				
	935				
	948				
	3031				
	3051				
	3052				
2	3064				
	3326				
	3708				*
	3721				
C	3770				

Kreinik - 027 Blending
Filament

Blue area indicates last row of
left section of design.
* Use 1 strand of floss and 1 strand
of Kreinik - 032 Blending Filament.
† Use 1 strand of floss and 1 strand
of Kreinik - 002 Blending Filament.
★ Use 1 strand of each floss color
listed.

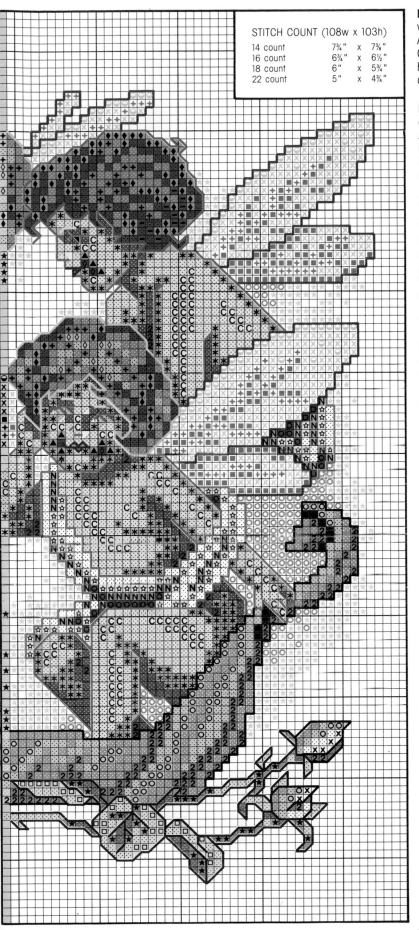

STITCH COUNT (108w x 103h)		
14 count	7¾"	x	7⅜"
16 count	6¾"	x	6½"
18 count	6"	x	5¾"
22 count	5"	x	4¾"

Morning Glory Melody in Frame (shown on page 48): The design was stitched over 2 fabric threads on an 18" x 15" piece of Antique White Belfast Linen (32 ct) using 2 strands of floss for Cross Stitch and 1 strand of floss or Kreinik Blending Filament for Half Cross Stitch and Backstitch, unless otherwise noted in the color key. It was custom framed.

Morning Glory Melody Sewing Basket (shown on page 45): The design was stitched over 2 fabric threads on a 16" square of Antique White Belfast Linen (32 ct) using 2 strands of floss for Cross Stitch and 1 strand of floss or Kreinik Blending Filament for Half Cross Stitch and Backstitch, unless otherwise noted in the color key.

Amounts of the following supplies will be determined by size of basket.

For basket, you will need a basket with handle (we used a 10½" dia. basket), tracing paper for lid pattern, batting for top of lid, two pieces of mounting board (slightly larger than outside edge of basket rim), fabric for lid backing, fabric for cording, ¼" dia. purchased cord, 1"w pregathered lace, four 15" lengths of ⅝"w ribbon, disappearing ink fabric marking pen, and clear-drying craft glue.

Cut a tracing paper pattern ¼" smaller than outside edge of basket rim, cutting notches for handle as needed.

For lid backing, draw around pattern on one piece of mounting board; cut out on drawn line. Place on basket and check fit; adjust pattern and mounting board as needed. Pin pattern to backing fabric, use fabric marking pen to draw around pattern, remove pattern and cut out 1" larger than drawn line (do not cut notches). Clip ½" into edge of backing fabric at 1" intervals. Center mounting board on backing fabric and cut 1" into backing fabric at center of one notch. Clip diagonally from end of 1" cut to inside corners of notch; repeat for remaining notch. Fold edges of backing fabric to back of mounting board and glue in place. Set lid backing aside.

For lid, draw around pattern on remaining piece of mounting board; cut out ¼" smaller than pattern for outer edge and cut out on drawn line for notches. Cut batting same size as mounting board; glue batting to mounting board. Center pattern on wrong side of stitched piece and pin pattern in place. Use fabric marking pen to draw around pattern, remove pattern and cut out 1" larger than drawn line (do not cut notches). Clip ½" into edge of stitched piece at 1" intervals. Position stitched piece on batting; cut 1" into stitched piece at center of one notch. Clip diagonally from end of 1" cut to inside corners of notch; repeat for remaining notch. Fold edges of stitched piece to back of mounting board and glue in place.

Cut a length of cord the circumference of lid plus 4"; cut a bias strip of fabric 2"w and same length as cord. Center cord on wrong side of bias strip; matching long edges, fold strip over cord. Use a zipper foot to baste along length of strip close to cord; cut length of cording in half. Referring to photo for placement, glue one length of cording to lid with 1" of cording extending beyond notches. On each end of cording remove 1" of basting and trim cord even with edge of notch. Turn loose ends of bias strip to back of lid and glue in place. Repeat for remaining length of cording. Cut a length of lace the circumference of lid plus 2"; cut length of lace in half. Press short edges of lace ½" to wrong side; refer to photo and glue lace to wrong side of cording. Repeat for remaining length of lace. Refer to photo and glue one length of ribbon to each side of one notch; trim ends as desired. Repeat with remaining lengths of ribbon and notch. Matching wrong sides and notches, glue lid and lid backing together.

Needlework adaptation by Carol Emmer.

Nostalgic Notions

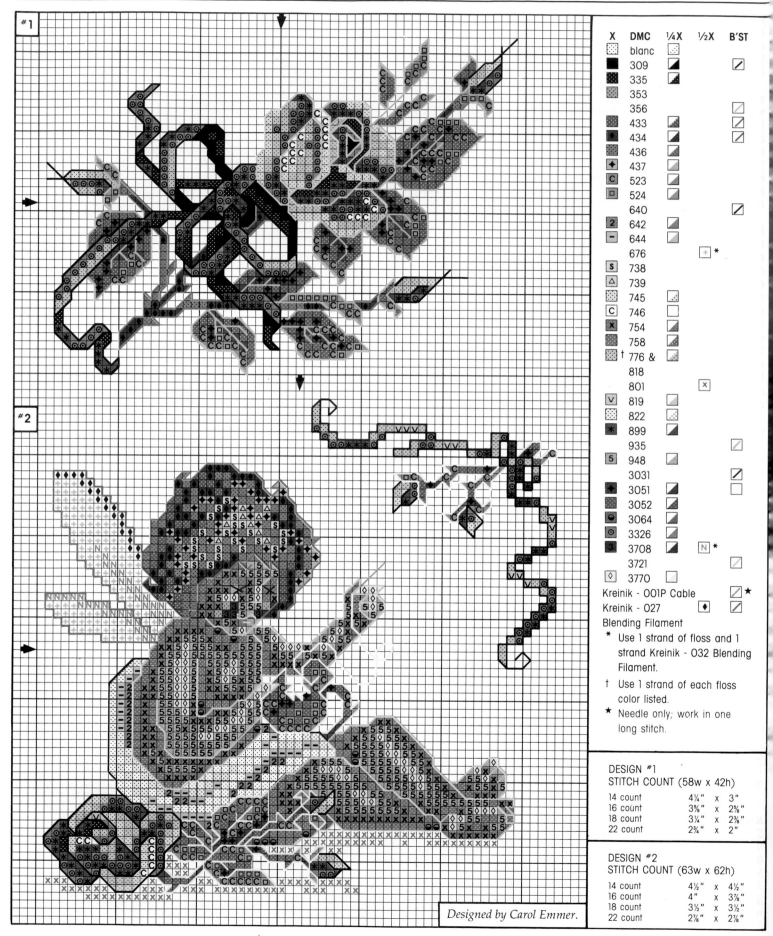

X	DMC	¼X	½X	B'ST
	blanc			
■	309			✓
■	335			
▨	353			
	356			✓
▨	433			✓
◆	434			✓
▨	436			
◆	437			
C	523			
▢	524			
	640			✓
2	642			
−	644			
	676		+*	
S	738			
△	739			
▨	745			
C	746			
✗	754			
▨	758			
▨ †	776 &			
	818			
	801		✗	
V	819			
	822			
✳	899			
	935			✓
5	948			
	3031			✓
■	3051			
▨	3052			
◉	3064			
◉	3326			
3	3708		N*	
	3721			✓
◇	3770			

Kreinik - 001P Cable ✓ ★

Kreinik - 027 ◆ ✓

Blending Filament

* Use 1 strand of floss and 1
  strand Kreinik - 032 Blending
  Filament.

† Use 1 strand of each floss
  color listed.

★ Needle only; work in one
  long stitch.

DESIGN #1
STITCH COUNT (58w x 42h)

14 count	4¼"	x	3"
16 count	3⅝"	x	2⅝"
18 count	3¼"	x	2⅜"
22 count	2¾"	x	2"

DESIGN #2
STITCH COUNT (63w x 62h)

14 count	4½"	x	4½"
16 count	4"	x	3⅞"
18 count	3½"	x	3½"
22 count	2⅞"	x	2⅞"

Designed by Carol Emmer.

Hanging Pincushion (shown on page 46): Design #1 was stitched over 2 fabric threads on a 9" x 10" piece of Antique White Belfast Linen (32 ct) using 2 strands of floss for Cross Stitch and 1 strand for Backstitch.

For pincushion, center design and trim stitched piece to measure 6½" x 5". You will also need a 6½" x 5" piece of fabric for backing, 21" length of purchased cording with attached seam allowance, 6½" length of 2"w lace, six 4" lengths of ⅛" dia. strung pearls for loops, two 10" lengths of ⅝"w ribbon for bows, and 12" length of 1/16"w ribbon and two 12" lengths of ⅛" dia. strung pearls for hanger.

If needed, trim seam allowance of cording to ½". Matching raw edges, pin cording to right side of stitched piece making a ⅜" clip in seam allowance of cording at corners. Ends of cording should overlap approximately 2"; pin overlapping end out of the way. Starting 2" from beginning end of cording and ending 4" from overlapping end, baste cording to stitched piece. On overlapping end of cording, remove 2½" of basting; fold end of fabric back and trim cord so that it meets beginning end of cord. Fold end of fabric under ½"; wrap fabric over beginning end of cording. Finish basting cording to stitched piece.

Matching right sides and leaving an opening for turning, use a zipper foot and ½" seam allowance to sew stitched piece and backing fabric together. Trim seam allowances diagonally at corners; turn pincushion right side out carefully pushing corners outward. Stuff pincushion with polyester fiberfill and blind stitch opening closed.

Press short edges of lace ½" to wrong side. Refer to photo and blind stitch lace to bottom edge of pincushion.

For pearl loops, use three 4" lengths of strung pearls and bring all ends together to form 3 loops. Refer to photo and tack loops to one top corner of pincushion. Tie one length of ⅝"w ribbon in a bow and trim ends as desired; tack bow over ends of loops. Repeat with remaining 4" lengths of strung pearls and ⅝"w ribbon for remaining top corner of pincushion.

For hanger, use 12" lengths of strung pearls and 1/16"w ribbon, align ends; refer to photo and tack ends to back of pincushion at one top corner. Refer to photo and twist strung pearls and ribbon together. Tack ends to back of pincushion at remaining top corner.

Needlework Organizer (shown on page 47): Design #2 was stitched over 2 fabric threads on an 11" square of Antique White Belfast Linen (32 ct) using 2 strands of floss for Cross Stitch and 1 strand of floss or Kreinik Blending Filament for Half Cross Stitch and Backstitch, unless otherwise noted in the color key.

For organizer, you will need a 5" square of mounting board, 5" square of batting, 2" x 23" bias strip of coordinating fabric for cording, 23" length of ¼" dia. purchased cord, ¾ yard of 44/45" reversible quilted fabric, ½ yard of heavyweight clear vinyl, 4¼ yards of ⅜"w double fold bias tape, sewing thread to match quilted fabric and bias tape, clear-drying craft glue, tracing paper, fabric marking pencil, and assorted laces, ribbons, trims, floral motifs cut from fabric, buttons, and pearls.

To mount stitched piece, glue batting to mounting board. Center stitched piece on batting and fold edges of stitched piece to back of mounting board; glue in place. For cording, center cord on wrong side of bias strip; matching long edges, fold strip over cord. Use a zipper foot to baste along length of strip close to cord. Starting 2" from beginning of cording and at bottom center of stitched piece, glue cording to back of stitched piece; stop 3" from overlapping end of cording.

On overlapping end of cording, remove 2½" of basting; fold end of fabric back and trim cord so that it meets beginning end of cord. Fold end of fabric under ½"; wrap fabric over beginning end of cording. Finish gluing cording to stitched piece.

(**Note:** Determine which side of the quilted fabric will be the outside of the organizer, this will be called the right side of fabric.)

From quilted fabric cut a 10½" x 13" piece for back (A), two 13¾" x 13" pieces for sides (B), and a 10½" x 8¾" piece for pocket (C). From vinyl cut a 10½" x 6" piece for pocket (D) and two 9" x 13" pieces for side pockets (E). To round corners of side pieces (B's), fold tracing paper in half and place fold on dashed line of Flap Pattern (page 95); trace pattern onto tracing paper. Cut out pattern; unfold and press flat. Refer to Diagram for remainder of instructions. Place pattern along one short edge of one B with edges aligned. Use fabric marking pencil to draw around rounded corners; remove pattern and cut out on drawn lines. Repeat for remaining B.

(**Note:** To sew vinyl, layer vinyl between 2 pieces of tracing paper to prevent presser foot from dragging; tear away paper after sewing.)

For pockets C, D, and E's, bind one long edge of each piece. Matching raw edges, place D on right side of C. Topstitch through both layers 3" from left edge. Bind top short end of A. Matching raw edges, place C/D on wrong side of A. Bind bottom short end through all thicknesses. Matching raw edges, place one E on wrong side of one B. Beginning at one corner, and working across long end to rounded corners, bind through all thicknesses around to remaining corner. Repeat with remaining E and B.

Press outside edge (with rounded corners) of one B to wrong side along fold line; stitch ¼" from folded edge through all layers. Repeat with remaining B. Matching wrong sides and raw edges, place one B/E on A/C/D and bind raw edges through all thicknesses on right side. Repeat with remaining B/E.

Refer to photo to fold organizer and sew 12" lengths of ribbon to organizer; trim ends as desired. Referring to photo for placement suggestions, glue laces, ribbons, trims, floral motifs, and stitched piece to front of organizer as desired; sew buttons and pearls to organizer as desired.

Diagram

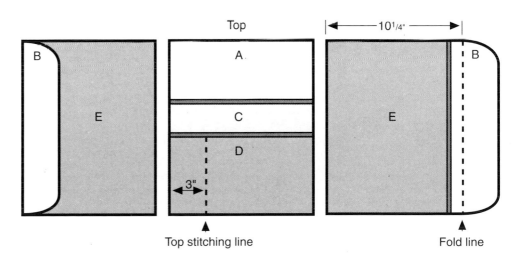

Nostalgic Notions

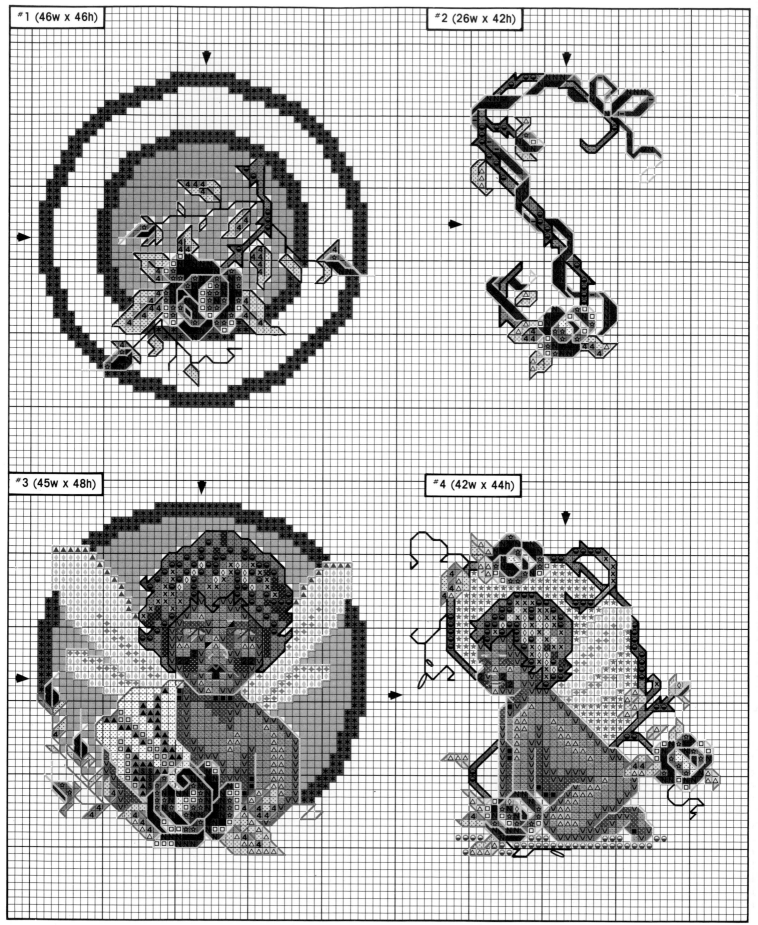

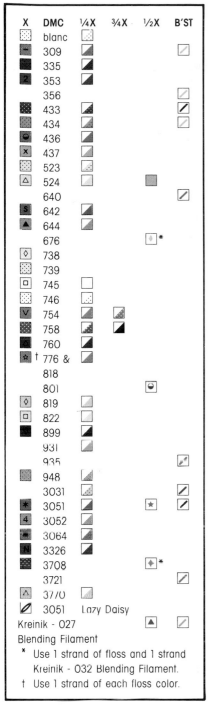

X	DMC	¼X	¾X	½X	B'ST
■	blanc	■			
−	309	■			/
■	335	■			
2	353	■			
	356				/
■	433	■			/
■	434	■			/
●	436	■			
×	437	■			
■	523	■			
△	524	■		■	
	640				/
S	642	■			
▲	644	■			
	676			◇*	
◇	738				
■	739				
□	745	□			
■	746	■			
V	754	■	■		
■	758	■	■		
■	760	■			
☆ †	776 & 818	■			
	801			■	
◇	819	■			
□	822	■			
■	899	■			
	931	■			
	935				/
■	948	■			
	3031	■			/
*	3051	■		★	/
4	3052	■			
■	3064	■			
N	3326	■			
■	3708			◆*	
	3721				/
△	3770	■			
⁄	3051	Lazy Daisy			
	Kreinik - 027 Blending Filament			▲	/

* Use 1 strand of floss and 1 strand Kreinik - 032 Blending Filament.

† Use 1 strand of each floss color.

Rose Pincushion (shown on page 44): Design #1 was stitched over 2 fabric threads on a 9" square of Antique White Belfast Linen (32 ct) using 2 strands of floss for Cross Stitch and 1 strand for Half Cross Stitch and Backstitch.

For pincushion, center design and trim stitched piece to measure 6" dia. circle. You will also need two 6" dia. circles of fabric for lining and backing, 4" dia. round Shaker box, 3½" x 13" fabric strip to cover sides of box, 4½" dia. circle of felt to cover bottom of box, 12½" length of 1"w pregathered lace, 12½" length of ⅜"w ribbon, 12" length of ⅜"w ribbon for bow, ½" dia. button, clear-drying craft glue, and polyester fiberfill.

To cover sides of box, clip ⅝" into one long edge of fabric strip at 1" intervals. Beginning at center back and placing clipped edge of strip 1" below lower edge of box, glue strip to sides of box. Fold clipped edge of strip to bottom of box and glue; fold upper edge of fabric strip to inside of box and glue. Center felt circle on bottom of box and glue in place. Refer to photo and glue lace and ribbon to box.

Baste lining fabric to wrong side of stitched piece close to raw edges. Matching right sides and leaving an opening for turning, use a ½" seam allowance to sew stitched piece and backing fabric together. Trim seam allowances and clip curves as needed; turn pincushion right side out. Stuff pincushion firmly with polyester fiberfill and blind stitch opening closed. Insert in box; refer to photo and glue bow and button to pincushion.

Nostalgic Notions Wreath (shown on page 48): Design #1 was stitched over 2 fabric threads on a 9" square of Antique White Belfast Linen (32 ct) using 2 strands of floss for Cross Stitch and 1 strand for Half Cross Stitch and Backstitch. It was inserted in a 4" dia. wooden embroidery hoop; fringe edges of fabric ¼" and attach to a decorated 19" dia. wreath.

Chatelaine (shown on page 46): Complete scissors case and needle case following instructions below. Referring to photo, blind stitch scissors case to one end of a 32" length of 1"w ribbon; blind stitch needle case to remaining end of ribbon.

Scissors Case (shown on page 46): Design #2 was stitched over 2 fabric threads on an 8" x 9" piece of Antique White Belfast Linen (32 ct) using 2 strands of floss for Cross Stitch and 1 strand for Backstitch.

For scissors case, you will need tracing paper, 8" x 9" piece of Belfast Linen for backing, two 8" x 9" pieces of fabric for lining, 2" x 12" bias strip of coordinating fabric for cording, 12" length of ¼" dia. purchased cord, 16" length of ¼"w ribbon, ⅜" dia. button, and fabric marking pencil.

Trace scissors case pattern (page 96) onto tracing paper; cut out pattern. Refer to photo to position pattern on wrong side of stitched piece and pin pattern in place. Use fabric marking pencil to draw around pattern, remove pattern. Cut out on drawn line; using stitched piece as pattern, cut out one piece from backing fabric and two pieces from lining fabric.

For cording, center cord on wrong side of bias strip; matching long edges, fold strip over cord. Use zipper foot to baste along length of strip close to cord; trim seam allowance to ¼". Referring to photo for placement, match raw edges and baste cording to right side of stitched piece with cording extended 1" beyond top edges.

Matching right sides and leaving top edge open, use a ¼" seam allowance to sew stitched piece and backing fabric together; clip curves and turn scissors case right side out. On each end of cording remove 1" of basting, trim cord even with top edge of scissors case. Turn loose ends of bias strip to inside of scissors case and blind stitch in place. Press top edges ¼" to wrong side. Matching right sides and leaving top edge open, use a ⅜" seam allowance to sew lining fabric together; trim seam allowance close to stitching. **Do not turn lining right side out.** Press top edges of lining ¼" to wrong side. With wrong sides facing, place lining inside scissors case; blind stitch in place.

Fold ribbon in half matching short ends. Refer to photo to blind stitch fold to inside of scissors case backing. Refer to photo and sew button to scissors case front.

Needle Case (shown on page 46): Design #4 was stitched over 2 fabric threads on a 12" x 8" piece of Antique White Belfast Linen using 2 strands of floss for Cross Stitch and 1 strand for Half Cross Stitch, Backstitch, and Lazy Daisy Stitch, unless otherwise noted in the color key. Fold fabric in half lengthwise, center design on right half of fabric.

For needle case, you will need 7½"x 3½" piece of fabric for lining, 26" bias strip of coordinating fabric for cording, 26" length of ¼" dia. purchased cord, 2" x 2½" piece of felt, two 8" lengths of ¼"w ribbon, and clear-drying craft glue.

With design centered vertically, trim fabric to 7½"x 3½" with design ⅞" from right edge of fabric. Center cord on wrong side of bias strip; matching long edges, fold strip over cord. Use a zipper foot to baste along length of strip close to cord; trim seam allowance to ¼". Matching raw edges, pin cording to right side of stitched piece. Ends of cording should overlap approximately 2"; pin overlapping end out of the way. Starting 2" from beginning end of cording and ending 4" from overlapping end, baste cording to right side of stitched piece. On overlapping end of cording, remove 2½" of basting; fold end of fabric back and trim cord so that it meets beginning end of cord. Fold end of fabric under ½"; wrap fabric over beginning end of cording. Finish basting cording to stitched piece.

Matching right sides and leaving an opening for turning, use a ¼" seam allowance to sew stitched piece and lining fabric together. Trim seam allowances diagonally at corners; turn needle case right side out carefully pushing corners outward and blind stitch opening closed. Matching short edges fold in half and press; open needle case and machine sew through all layers along fold line. Open needle case and center felt piece on right half of lining; glue top ½" of felt piece in place. Refer to photo and blind stitch one length of ribbon to lining on needle case front, repeat for remaining length of ribbon and needle case back.

Fairy in Standing Hoop (shown on page 49): Design #3 was stitched over 2 fabric threads on a 9" square of Antique White Belfast Linen (32 ct) using 2 strands of floss for Cross Stitch and 1 strand of floss or Kreinik Blending Filament for Half Cross Stitch and Backstitch, unless otherwise noted in color key. It was inserted in a 4" dia. standing wooden embroidery hoop, fringe edges of fabric ¼".

Designed by Carol Emmer.

GENERAL INSTRUCTIONS

WORKING WITH CHARTS

How to Read Charts: Each of the designs is shown in chart form. Each colored square on the chart represents one Cross Stitch or one Half Cross Stitch. Each colored triangle on the chart represents one One-Quarter Stitch or one Three-Quarter Stitch. Black or colored dots represent French Knots. Colored ovals represent Lazy Daisy Stitches. The black or colored straight lines on the chart indicate Backstitch. When a French Knot, Lazy Daisy Stitch, or Backstitch covers a square, the symbol is omitted.

Each chart is accompanied by a color key. This key indicates the color of floss to use for each stitch on the chart. The headings on the color key are for Cross Stitch (**X**), DMC color number (**DMC**), Quarter Stitch (**¼X**), Three-Quarter Stitch (**¾X**), Half Cross Stitch (**½X**), and Backstitch (**B'ST**). Color key columns should be read vertically and horizontally to determine type of stitch and floss color.

Where to Start: The horizontal and vertical centers of each charted design are shown by arrows. You may start at any point on the charted design, but be sure the design will be centered on the fabric. Locate the center of fabric by folding in half, top to bottom and again left to right. On the charted design, count the number of squares (stitches) from the center of the chart to where you wish to start. Then from the fabric's center, find your starting point by counting out the same number of fabric threads (stitches). (**Note:** To work over two fabric threads, count out twice the number of fabric threads.)

How To Determine Finished Size: The finished size of your design will depend on the **thread count per inch** of the fabric being used. To determine the finished size of the design on different fabrics, divide the number of squares (stitches) in the width of the charted design by the thread count of the fabric. For example, a charted design with a width of 80 squares worked on 14 count Aida will yield a design 5¾" wide. Repeat for the number of squares (stitches) in the height of the charted design. (**Note:** To work over two fabric threads, divide the number of squares by one-half the thread count.) Then add the amount of background you want plus a generous amount for finishing.

STITCH DIAGRAMS

Counted Cross Stitch (X): Work one Cross Stitch to correspond to each colored square on the chart. For horizontal rows, work stitches in two journeys (**Fig. 1**). For vertical rows, complete each stitch as shown (**Fig. 2**). When working over two fabric threads, work Cross Stitch as shown in **Fig. 3**. When the chart shows a Backstitch crossing a colored square (**Fig. 4**), a Cross Stitch should be worked first; then the Backstitch (**Fig. 9 or 10**) should be worked on top of the Cross Stitch.

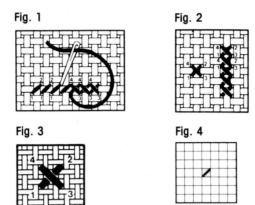

Fig. 1   **Fig. 2**

Fig. 3   **Fig. 4**

Quarter Stitch (¼X and ¾X): Quarter Stitches are denoted by triangular shapes of color on the chart and on the color key. Come up at 1 (**Fig. 5**); then split fabric thread to go down at 2. When stitches 1-4 are worked in the same color, the resulting stitch is called a Three-Quarter Stitch (**¾X**). **Fig. 6** shows the technique for Quarter Stitch when working over two fabric threads.

Fig. 5   **Fig. 6**

Half Cross Stitch (½X): This stitch is one journey of the Cross Stitch and is worked from lower left to upper right as shown in **Fig. 7**. When working over two fabric threads, work Half Cross Stitch as shown in **Fig. 8**.

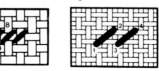

Fig. 7   **Fig. 8**

Backstitch (B'ST): For outline detail, Backstitch (shown on chart and on color key by black or colored straight lines) should be worked after the design has been completed (**Fig. 9**). When working over two fabric threads, work Backstitch as shown in **Fig. 10**.

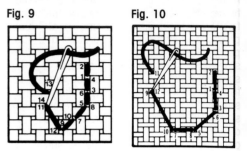

Fig. 9   **Fig. 10**

French Knot: Bring needle up at 1. Wrap floss once around needle and insert needle at 2, holding end of floss with non-stitching fingers (**Fig. 11**). Tighten knot; then pull needle through fabric, holding floss until it must be released. For larger knot, use more strands; wrap only once.

Fig. 11

Lazy Daisy Stitch: Bring needle up at 1 and make a loop. Go down at 1 and come up at 2, keeping floss below point of needle (**Fig. 12**). Pull needle through and go down at 2 to anchor loop, completing stitch. (**Note:** To support stitches, it may be helpful to go down in edge of next fabric thread when anchoring loop.)

Fig. 12

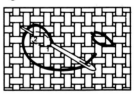

Nun Stitch: Fabric threads should be pulled tightly together to create an opening in the fabric around the stitch. Figs. show placement of stitch but do not show pulling of the fabric threads. Keep tension even throughout work.

This continuous edging stitch is worked from top to bottom. Each stitch is worked twice; stitches 1-2 and 3-4 are over the same fabric threads (**Fig. 13**). Come up at 1 and pull tightly toward 2; then go down at 2 and pull tightly toward 1. Work stitch 3-4 over the same fabric threads. Work stitches 5-16 in same manner (**Fig. 13**). Continue working in the same manner to corner, ending with a stitch worked in the same manner as stitches 13-16. To turn corner, come up at 17 and then go down at 18. Work stitch 19-20 over the same fabric threads as shown in **Fig. 14**. Turn fabric, work stitches 21-24 in same manner (**Fig. 15**). Continue working in the same manner around.

Fig. 13   **Fig. 14**

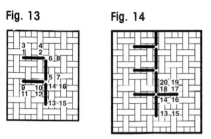

Fig. 15

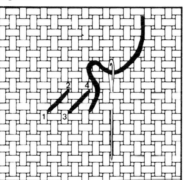

STITCHING TIPS

Working Over Two Fabric Threads: Use the sewing method instead of the stab method when working over two fabric threads. To use the sewing method, keep your stitching hand on the right side of the fabric (instead of stabbing the fabric with the needle and taking your stitching hand to the back of the fabric to pick up the needle). With the sewing method, you take the needle down and up with one stroke instead of two. To add support to stitches, it is important that the first Cross Stitch is placed on the fabric with stitch 1-2 beginning and ending where a vertical fabric thread crosses over a horizontal fabric thread (**Fig. 16**). When the first stitch is in the correct position, the entire design will be placed properly, with vertical fabric threads supporting each stitch.

Fig. 16

Attaching Beads: Refer to chart for bead placement and sew bead in place using a fine needle that will pass through bead. Bring needle up at 1, run needle through bead then down at 2 making a Half Cross Stitch (**Fig. 17**). Secure floss on back or move to next bead as shown in **Fig. 17**.

Fig. 17

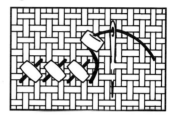

Instructions tested and photo items made by Junel Akins, Debbie Barrett, Marsha Besancon, Rhonda Bielefeldt, Carrie Clifford, Karen Gamble, Muriel Hicks, Joyce Holland, Connie Irby, Pat Johnson, Mimi Jones, Arthur Jungnickel, Vanessa Kiihnl, Phyllis Lundy, Colleen Moline, Margaret Mosoloy, Ray Ellen Odle, Dave Ann Pennington, Mary Phinney, Sandy Pigue, Carol Reed, Gail Sharp, Debra Smith, Amy Taylor, Mary Tedford, and Marie Williford

Flap Pattern

Continued on page 96.

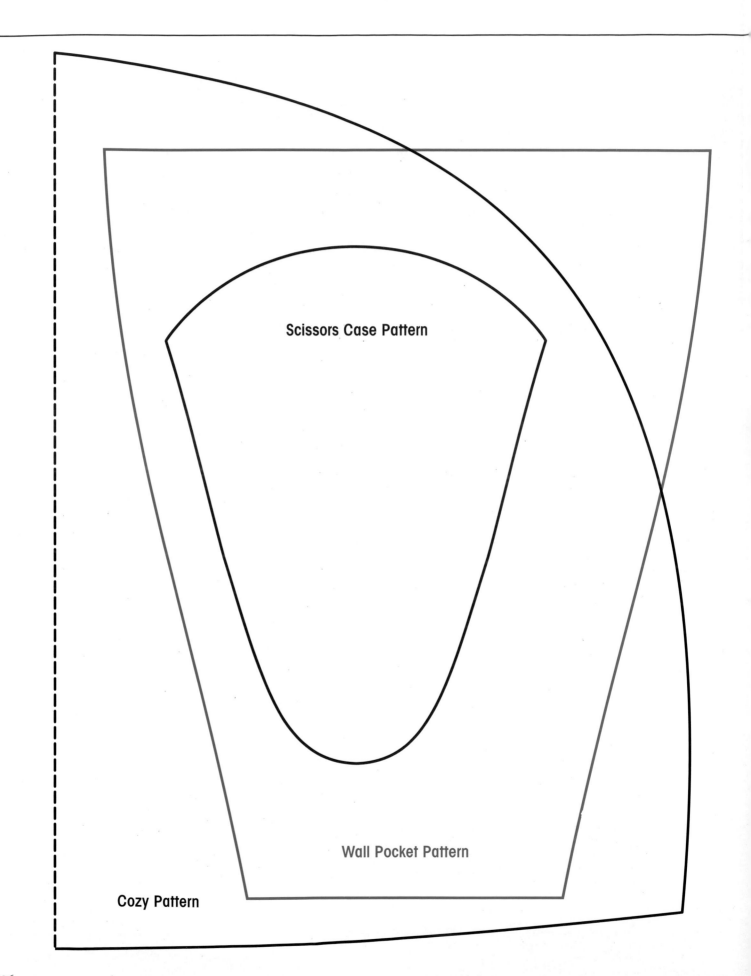

Scissors Case Pattern

Wall Pocket Pattern

Cozy Pattern